MW01452813

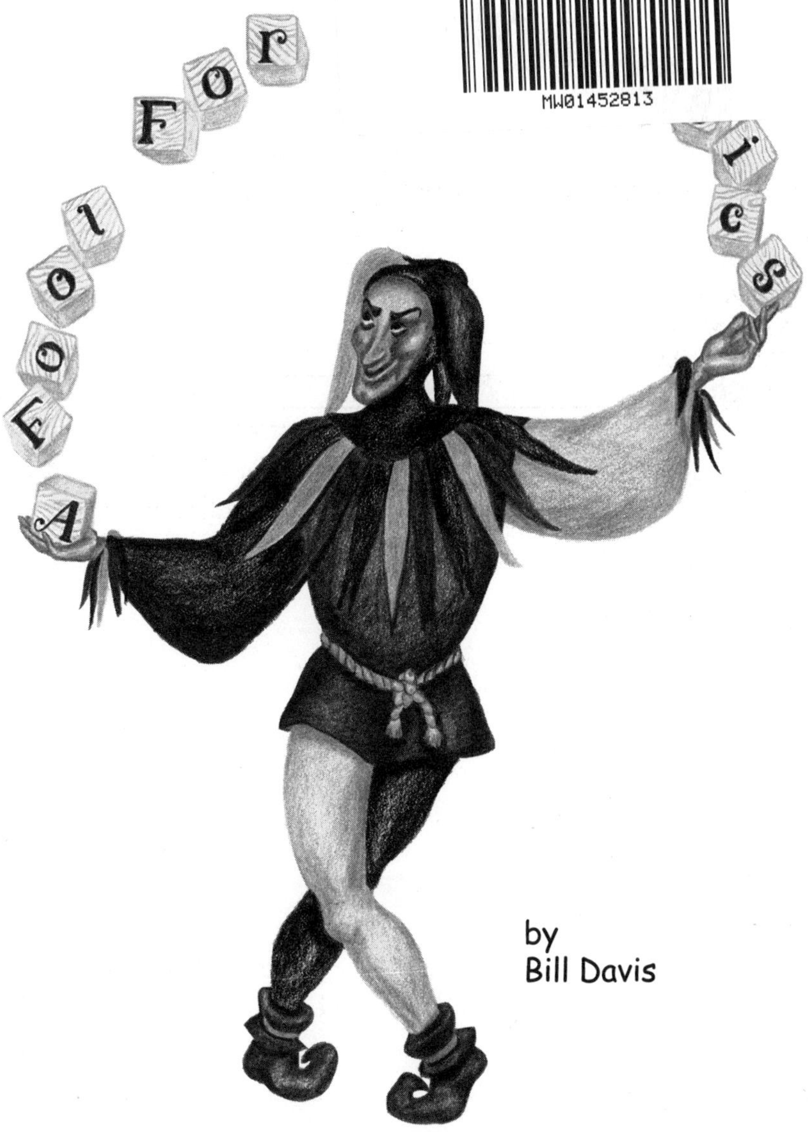

by
Bill Davis

A Collection of Debate and Individual Events Essays for High School Coaches and Students

Clark Publishing
Since 1948

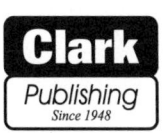

Developing Communication Skills

Copyright © 1997, Clark Publishing, Inc.
All rights reserved. No part of this book may be reproduced, stored in a retrieval system, or transmitted in any form or by any means, electronic, mechanical, photocopying, recording, or otherwise, without prior written permission from the publisher.

Published By,
Clark Publishing, Inc.
P.O. Box 19240
Topeka, Kansas 66619-0240
(913) 862-0218
(800) 845-1916 in U.S.

Designed by **Todd Ricardo Kinney**

Cover Art and Illustrations by **Michèle Klosterman-Jackson**
Layout by **Todd Ricardo Kinney** and **Lara Rae Saville**

First Printing, First Edition
Proudly printed and bound in Kansas, USA by Gilliland Printing

ISBN 0-931054-47-8

Dedication

This work is dedicated to Charles Fulcher, who got me into this mess.
Thanks, Coch!

About The Author

Bill Davis was a terrible debater in high school, a slimy and lazy debater in college, and a disc jockey in his youth. He has now paid for his sins by sixteen years of teaching apparent clones of himself.

Acknowledgements

Many thanks to James Copeland for allowing my columns to be a part of *The Rostrum* magazine. Special thanks to Diana Carlin of Clark Publishing, Inc. for helping make this book a reality.

Introduction

by Mahlon Coop
Blue Valley Northwest High School Debate

The way I had it figured, listening to Him over the years, I was Yang to Bill Davis's Ying. I made a big mistake.

I mean, if you ever had a question about debate theory, debate technique, or then, basic forensics stuff, anyone around here would have the good sense to say "ask Bill Davis, see what he says."

I kept supposing they would then say, "and then, oh, yeah, don't forget to ask Mahlon Coop too."

Well, that's the last time you will hear MY name in this book. And deservedly so. Even though Bill Davis once insisted on calling me his debate "guru," I have learned to discover that Bill Davis *knows it*.

What I seem to begin to sense is right, or lean toward, or am in a state of pondering, Bill Davis has apprehended, hands down, and found the language for — and damn him! He's clever and entertaining to boot. But the thing I really love/hate about this book, is that Bill Davis knows how to "Incremental You."

By that, I mean, there **has got** to be **one** essay in this book that "works" for either teacher or student of forensics or debate. (By the way, **don't** start reading this book at the beginning, scan the Table of Contents, create your own order based on interest or need, and see if I ain't right). And once that one essay brings you **the** insight suddenly, you will find another essay that "works", and then the wisdom of another collects around your consciousness. Suddenly, you find yourself feeding off this book, each essay a meal, each meal making you hungry for another. O, what a tasting.

I have never known a debate/forensics coach to take such an Aristotelian–analytical–breakdown approach to basic debate and forensics theory, then, separate the wheat from the chaff, and then, find such lively, understandable ways to make it engaging, holistic, and Platonic, particularly to those (i.e. students) who must **do** something with the knowledge. The gulf between the normal Knowledge Textbook and the unique High School Mind of Application defies most ships and oil tankers I know. Much gets sunk, or lost, or worse, spills to cause damage beyond our abilities to assess in the movement of "our" particular wisdoms to "their" applications.

I get to speak from experience. I have witnessed many of Bill Davis's student-debater-forensicators. After watching them, I'm convinced that Aristotle and Plato would have shook hands and then bought each other breakfast at Denny's, and have eaten well.

Eat well. You cannot order wrongly no matter where you start in this book. Your only mistake will be in not becoming a repeat customer — because others most certainly will. This book moves beyond the wisdom of the debate/forensics chef, where knowledge becomes both food and a beautiful, learning wind-chime.

Introduction

Table Of Contents

Introduction
by Mahlon Coop iv

Policy Debate
Answering Generics 3
A Brutal Affirmative 8
The First Affirmative Rebuttal 17
The Second Negative Rebuttal 23
In a Clearing Stands a Boxes 29
Colleague Calamity 33
Natty Bumppo's Debate Advice 37
Division of Labor? Sounds Like Work to Me 41
I Love to Tell the Stories 49

Individual Events
The Fundamentals of Interp 57
Too Dumb to Breathe 63
It's in the Bag 67
Off the Subject 71
I Can See You Naked 77
How Interp Could Learn From Baseball 81
Statue! Gresunheit! 87

Lincoln-Douglas Debate
Diogenes Visits the Coaches' Lounge 93
Keeping Your Cool 99
The Last Words of Socrates 103
Have Gun, Will Gavel 107
The Longest Commandment 111
Fundamentals of the Argumentative Events 115

Critical Thinking and Lateral Thinking

Chapter 1- Why Iz Evryboddy Always Pickin' On Me? 123
Chapter 2- Playin' In the Sun With My Reverse Barometer 131
Chapter 3- Assume Nothing 139
Chapter 4 - In Which the Author Becomes Rather Kinky 147
Chapter 5- Where the Good Arguments Are 153
Chapter 6- Po' Li'l Me 159
Chapter 7- More Exercises than Jane Fonda 167
Chapter 8- Building the Perfect Beast 175

Pot Pourers

Gomer 183
Squad Spirit 189
Good Grief! 193
You Gotta Know the Rules 197
The Forensics Songbook 201
A Chronicle of the Plague Year 205
The Director of Humanity 211

Table Of Contents   vii

Policy Debate

Answering Generics
or
The Maltese Malthus
(originally published January 1991, revised July 1995)

Some private detectives chase divorce cases. Others move to Hawaii to become TV stars. Me? I'm a debate detective. I'm the best. I flow fast, talk faster, and my ears pack 20-20 hearing. My name? It's Lincoln Douglas. I can't help my parents' taste.

But I was bored. I hadn't had much business over the summer months, and now that the first tournaments were under way I had a lot of time on top of the ink on my hands.

So, I was in the bathroom of my office rinsing out my briefs when the john door opened and in stepped a dame. She had hair the hue of a catalog case, skin the color of a cream colored legal pad, and the figure of a two drawer file box ready to spill.

She looked at me. I looked at her. I spoke. "Lady this is my private john. A little privacy, huh?"

Later, as I emerged into my office she was plopped on my desk, nervously chewing on her multicolored pen. For a long time I said nothing. She finished her prep time.

"It's my affirmative case, it's gone."

"What do you mean, gone."

She giggled. "Just what I said. I took it to the first tournament and it disappeared in three rooms. The negative got up, and it just disappeared."

"You suspect anybody. Like your colleague?"

She snorted, and a little fleck of spit lodged itself to her lower lip. She certainly seemed genuine. I poured her a fifth response and she gratefully spilled it all over her dress. Only a debater would be so uncoordinated.

Finally, she spoke again. "No," she babbled, "I know who did it. It was...the Generic Gang!"

A hush fell over the room. I think it was because neither of us was talking. "You mean 'Nasty' Nukes, 'Gonzo' Growth, and 'Mickey' Malthus?"

"Yes," she gasped.

"Sugar, they're all the same. Bad eggs. But you'll get over it. There are other affirmative cases. I can get you a good deal on an Aliens Disco Death case."

"No!," she cried, "I want my old affirmative back! I just need to disprove the Generic Gang!"

I chortled. "You mean carry dirt on Gramm, Rudman, and those other jokers? That's a lot of evidence to spew out in a rebuttal, Precious. Can you handle it?" I leered at her.

"Of course not! I can't talk fast! Look at these!" Those lovely lips parted to display more twisted metal than a debate van after a sharp curve. "Some debaters give road maps before their speeches, I have to pass out towels."

"Well then, maybe you better figure out how to damage the Generic Gang in the cross-ex, so that you can save time in the rebuttal."

"Tell me how, Douglas."

"Call me Link, babe. Before you can disprove the Generic Gang, you have to have Motive and Mechanism."

She goggled. "What? What kind of debate theory is this? What happened to Brink, Impact and Uniqueness?"

"That's the Law Firm down the hall. Now pipe down. This is different. It's analysis. Ever heard of it?" I ignored her pouting.

"The first thing you do in the cross-ex is establish quick labels for each subpoint of the generic that you are going to take out. Due to the speed of the second negative, merely because most second negatives who run generics aren't very good anyway, what you have on your flow and what the judge has may be different. Unlike current strategies, it is better that you and the judge agree on what was said so you aren't wasting your time talking about something that the Guy with the ballot doesn't have down. Clear?" She nodded, but she obviously wasn't enthused.

Suddenly, I kissed her hard on the lips. She drew back, and popped me one right in the chops. I grinned as I sopped up the blood. "Now you know how to beat the Generic Gang."

"No, now I know you're crazy. Why did you do that?"

"I was making my point about motives and mechanisms. As I was laying the Big One on your kisser, you didn't know what to do at first, right?"

"You can say that again. But I obviously didn't have the same motives as you. And as for your mechanism, you'd better see your dentist, Big Mouth."

"I said call me Link. And that is the problem with the Generic Gang. It confuses actions with mechanisms."

"They're not the only ones who are confused. Keep talking."

"Take the Malthus D/A. That old chestnut has been around all these years because of two points. First, it is based on the fact that populations have been expanding for centuries, and second, because the eventual impact of expanding population is extinction. But the problem is this — motives are constantly changing as they are encountered by other motives. People have been creating more people because it has been advantageous for them to do so. As world population grows, the costs of having children will grow higher, and the population rate will slow down."

Answering Generics

She had begun to flow, reluctantly. "So your point is that unless the negative can show a motive that ultimately outweighs the motive to continue living, they can't show impact."

I patted her head. "Exactly. And now for mechanism. Current events tell us that as population growth becomes more apparently undesirable, governments respond with birth control, or even better, programs that make life easier if people don't have children. In other words, alternatives — mechanisms — exist short of just waiting to see the food chain collapse."

She sucked noisily on her pen. "Great. But how do I prove this without evidence?"

"Evidence? Who said anything about that yet? The burden lies with the negative, because that's who brought it up. You demand the evidence for the motives and the lack of alternative mechanisms in the cross-ex. If they cannot produce it, the argument dies for lack of a crucial internal link."

She blew on her smoking pen. "So what was the motive and mechanism business?"

"You never figured that out? Motive means that generics must prove that the main actors that cause the disad's impact are so motivated that nothing will change their course, not even prospective disaster. And Mechanism means that there are no other lesser options that these highly motivated actors may take. Think about it. The very fact that effects topicality is so popular this year is a sign that Motive and Mechanism are going to be very difficult to prove for a brain dead negative team that hasn't done it's research."

She gnawed so tightly on her pen that the plastic split with a crack nastier than a two girls' champ round cross-ex. "But if this Motives and Mechanisms stuff is so great, why don't all debaters run it?"

6   A Tool For Forensics — Policy Debate

"Everyone does, once in a while. But what most debaters forget is how to organize the analysis. Maybe some day the Good Guys will win and the Generic Gang will go away. And now, confess, Sweet-heart, you really aren't a debater."

She gasped, and then hurled her pen across the room. "Link, honey, how did you know?"

I grinned. "Because real debaters don't chew their pens. They compulsively twirl them."

She left, sobbing. Just another lovely interper, looking for a perfect HI.

A Brutal Affirmative

(unpublished)

I am often asked "what should a good affirmative do and what can it expect to accomplish?" I then answer myself — "Well, what is a good affirmative, anyway?"

Here is one. It was advocated by the team of J.D. Liggett and Brian Mathey, and it won six of seven rounds at the state championship tournament in January 1995. I'll present it with footnotes for reasons why the speech is structured as it is, and perhaps it will model what I like best about affirmatives.

INS brutality case

"Welcome to the United States!
"You look suspicious. Are you here legally?
"I don't believe you. Show me some ID.
"Don't talk like that to me. I'll teach you a thing about respect for authority in this country!"

This scenario is all too common in the United States today. It is an all too common of an experience for people who are United states citizens who fall afoul of an arrogant agent of the Immigration and Naturalization Service. (A) Because Michelin Head (B) and I feel this is no way to regulate immigration, we stand **Resolved: that the United States government should substantially strengthen regulation of immigration to the United States.** (C)

We begin by calling your attention to the wording of the resolution. It demands that the affirmative team strengthen the regulation of immigration. This wording best fits, by context, the following definitions from the American Heritage Dictionary;

strengthen- to make strong or stronger
and
regulation- the act of regulating.

Therefore, the resolution demands that we make stronger the act of regulating immigration to the United States. (D)

The regulating to which we are subjecting these aliens and others unfortunate enough to be mistaken for aliens, is a violation of human rights. As we note in **Observation I Lawbreaking is never justified in enforcing the law**. For proof we turn to no less than Justice Brandeis, quoted in Basic Cases in Constitutional Law, 2nd edition, 1987 on page 259:

> **Our government is the potent, the omnipresent teacher. For good or ill, it teaches the whole people by its example. Crime is contagious. If the government becomes a lawbreaker, it breeds contempt for the law; it invites every man to become a law unto himself; it invites anarchy.** (E)

We will prove to you in our advantage structure that the Border Patrol regulates immigration with an iron fist. This regulation is intolerable, and we strengthen it by the following proposal.

Plan Plank I – Civilian review boards shall be established to review violations of basic human rights by the Border Patrol. These include the right to be safe in one's person and safe from attack from another.

The composition, administration and powers of these civilian review boards shall be modeled on the systems established in San Diego. The boards shall have the power of subpoena.

Plan Plank II – Funding shall be by diversion of funds now given to the internal review boards of the Border Patrol, which shall be abolished. Any additional funding shall be by general federal revenue. (F)

Plan Plank III – The usual stuff — legislative intent, fiat, and other jargon. (G)

Let's compare the present system of regulating immigration with the affirmative proposal. Presently, if any person is mistreated by the Border Patrol, the only means of appeal is to the INS itself, which routinely sides, no surprise, with the agent. We abolish these boards and substitute a civilian review board. The members of the board will be appointed by the President. The board will have investigators who will have the power to force appearances by witnesses and agents before hearings conducted by due process. We will read you evidence that these boards will substantially strengthen the regulation of immigration by improving the performance of the Border Patrol.(H)

Advantage: the regulation of immigration is substantially strengthened by restoring the Border Patrol to the ranks of the law

This will be clearly demonstrated through three subpoints(I)

Subpoint A: The Border Patrol is out of control

We observe two dimensions of this problem, beginning in Reason 1(J)

Reason 1: Border violence, violates the basic values of America

A representative from the State of California, Esteban E. Torres, testified(K) as follows before the subcommittee on International Law, Immigration and Refugees of the House of Representatives on August 5, 1992(L):

> Border violence, both the treatment of US citizens and the treatment of Mexican nationals in the United States, rightly deserves attention internationally and domestically. As a country we promote civil rights and human dignity. We have fought wars against those who preached and preyed on hate in the name of national unity. We must hold ourselves to the same standards both at home and abroad. At stake are the very qualities which made our country the leader that it is: compassion, empathy and respect for basic human rights. I do not condone nor excuse illegal entry into our country. However, violence and discrimination cannot be weapons for enforcement and control of our border.

Are these principles used in regulating immigration? We see the answer in Reason 2.

Reason 2: Violence by Border Patrol agents is routine.

I will present you three pieces of evidence.

1. (Read "first") Aryeh Neier, Executive Director of Human Rights Watch, testifies under oath before the same subcommittee. I point out the oath because no Border Patrol agent is currently required to testify under oath in any disciplinary hearing! Mr. Neier states:

   We conclude that Border Patrol agents in the field behave as if they are accountable to no one. Beatings, rough physical treatment, intimidation tactics, and verbal abuse are routine. Even more serious abuses, including unjustified shootings, torture and sexual abuse, are reported all too often.

2. (Read "secondly") the attitude of the agents is shown by Mario Moreno, executive director of the Diocesan Migrant and Refugee Services, testifying before the same subcommittee on September 27, 1993:

   Patterns of violence have emerged; INS agents have admittedly administered street justice to those who have either attempted to flee capture or who have challenged the authority of an officer. Supervisors tolerate and even encourage that behavior. In fact, as a striking example of the dehumanization of immigrants, border patrol agents commonly refer to undocumented immigrants as "tonks," the sound that a flashlight makes when it hits an immigrant on the head.

3. (Read "thirdly") the numbers from Rep. Torres, previously qualified:

   The Immigration Law Enforcement Monitoring Project reported that from May 1989 to May 1991, 392 persons reported 1,274 abuses in immigration law enforcement to the monitoring project. (M)

A Brutal Affirmative

What the Border Patrol does about this is demonstrated in Subpoint B

Subpoint B: The Border Patrol is not held accountable

Two reasons

I will read you two pieces of evidence here

Reason 1: There is no effective overseeing of the Border Patrol

Washington magazine, edition of May 13, 1993 reports on the America's Watch findings:

> **When those (disciplinary) procedures which have been generally hidden from the public were exposed, they confirmed what immigrant and human rights activists have been saying for years — that US Border Patrol agents are simply not accountable for abuses. The report charges that procedures for handling complaints are seriously flawed and virtually guarantee that abuses are under-reported. At many points in the process, it says, INS agents can pose obstacles and otherwise prevent action from being taken.**

Reason 2: The result leads to poor regulation by the Border patrol of its tasks.

Cecelia Munoz, Senior Immigration Policy Analyst, in hearings before the Subcommittee on Government Information, Justice and Agriculture testifies on March 30, 1993:

> A court in El Paso, Texas recently enjoined the Border Patrol from harassing individuals solely because they look Hispanic. The action came after students and faculty at Bowie High School were harassed, beaten, detained and chased by Border Patrol agents simply because of

their appearance and their Hispanic heritage. In addition, the Border Patrol agents searched the assistant football coach without probable cause, and pointed a gun at the head football coach. These events are sadly typical of the Hispanic American experience with immigration law enforcement; such activities not only do nothing to control immigration, they undermine the credibility and effectiveness of the entire enforcement process.

The solution is to adopt civilian overseeing of the Border Patrol, and the results are noted in subpoint C.

Subpoint C: Civilian review Boards substantially strengthen regulation of immigration to the United States

Two reasons,

Reason 1: Civilian review boards work

Aryeh Neier, previously cited, demonstrates how they solve:

> Currently, more than half the major cities in the United States have some mechanism with varying degrees of independence for reviewing complaints against the police. Close to half the cities that have such systems have independent staff to investigate complaints. We believe that the experience of the cities that have such procedures warrants the call for the establishment of an independent board of review of complaints against the Border Patrol, and that, given the difficulty currently in persuading victims of abuse to come forward because of the fear of reprisals, such an independent board is particularly required in the case of Border Patrol abuses.

We conclude with the strange case of the status quo in reason 2(N):

Reason 2: The changes instituted this past year by the Clinton administration admit everything and change nothing.

The San Diego Union Tribune reported on March 26, 1994 on p.5:

> **The Immigration and Naturalization service, which oversees the Border Patrol, last month approved the formation of a national panel, which will review complaints against agents and concerning procedures:** *The thirteen member panel will be composed of nine citizens, plus four members from the Justice Department, including at least one from the INS. The panel lacks the powers to subpoena witnesses, collect evidence and hire investigators.*

Welcome to the United States. Tonk. (O)

(A) This introduction certainly did what introductions are supposed to do — it got attention. A team that was to do very well at the national tournament, in fact, wasted cross-ex time by getting arrogant about it. "What is this introduction? D.I.?" "No," J.D. replied, "But my coach loves D.I." "Tell him this is debate, all right?" By becoming an arrogant villain, he lost one of the judges immediately. No doubt there are some who would say that the judge intervened, but that would be the same people who would have been just as obnoxious as the negative debater, so pfui!

(B) Inside joke. The original copy is full of notes from the debaters insulting each other, primarily to remind J.D. to watch his speed, because he has a speech defect.

(C) It is incredibly important that the resolution be delivered slowly and precisely. Many judges DO NOT KNOW THE RESOLUTION! (gasp!)

(D) The definitions of terms are necessary because the case is not the usual interpretation of the topic. That is why the topic is restated with the definitions inserted. The one debate lost was by topicality (2-1 decision)

(E) No your eyes do not deceive you. This will be the impact of the affirmative case — a lowly value.

(F) This is a very short affirmative plan. We have discovered that the longer the plan, the more suspicious the judge becomes of it.

(G) Yes, he said that. Six judges laughed. No negative comments on the ballots. Perhaps judges are getting tired of the jargon intended to spike out disads?

(H) This is the most important twenty-five seconds of the 1AC. Not only does it put the affirmative plan in perspective, but it also answers topicality. We have had judges tell us this is a waste of time, but then vote almost word for word with the explanation.

(I) Transitions are the best way that you can ensure that the judge will keep up with you, without needless repetition.

(J) A reason is much more reasonable than a "little."

(K) A verb inserted into a source makes it flow smoother, is more rhetorical, and gives the quote a punch. J.D, also had another copy of the speech, in which Brian inserted "joke verbs" like "moaned," "whined" and "expostulated". This is mostly for the grins of thinking what it would sound like, while in the throes of endless preparation for the tournament. But, with the right panel, they would have used them.

(L) This is not an NFL speech, so the title of the document is not in the source, nor the page number. This makes me uncomfortable, but it wasn't required, and the debaters "didn't have the time," so I agreed to leaving off the title. There was a copy of all the evidence with all the NFL requirements laying on the desk as J.D. read the speech. If asked, he would produce it.

(M) Why three pieces of evidence instead of three points? Read the evidence again (notice we said evidence and not cards). All three are necessary to prove the point. Three more subpoints could not do that more efficiently.

A Brutal Affirmative

(N) Here is the strategic point of the affirmative. The last point of a case is usually the one mishandled by the negative, therefore, if you want something to pull, here it is. Can you figure out why the point is critical?

(O) A brief conclusion, but still in the mode of the introduction. You may not like the affirmative case (I loved it.) But it does what an affirmative needs to do, and it does it with style.

The First Affirmative Rebuttal

or

Slow! Like It Says On Your Transcript!

(originally published November 1989. Revised July 1995)

Debate rules give the negative only one advantage; if the two speakers in the negative bloc can throw out enough arguments that the first affirmative rebuttal cannot answer them all, then the impact of the Unfair Speech, the last affirmative rebuttal, can be muted. This makes for very exciting (yawn!) debate. It's always enjoyable watching a negative try to end the debate eight minutes early. The so-called breakthrough of ballooning generic arguments is just the same strategy, except it attempts to end the debate in the 2NC instead of twelve minutes later. This is even more exciting.

Of course, affirmatives have seen the stupidity of this strategy, and have evolved reasonable ways to answer it. Well... you gotta remember, these are the same folks who invented the negative strategy. So, strategy for the well designed 1AR is to practice talking with dictionaries on your abdomen. I'm pretty sure we are in the middle of the era that will be regarded by our debating successors as the equivalent of Chinese foot binding.

There is no need to replace your tie after every tournament because it was soaked in spit (yours and your opponents). Tell the people who try to transform you into a freak of nature that there is a better way.

Preparation for the well-dressed 1AR is based on three principles. First, if the 1N is badly defeated then the number of arguments that need to be answered will be greatly decreased. Second, reading evidence is counterproductive in the 1AR. Third, the biggest waste of time in rebuttal comes from explaining your opponent's arguments.

How to wipe out the 1N

1. Choose a stock affirmative. The approach to 1N used by most debaters in high school is based on fear — that the prep time will run out and the 1N will be standing in his skivvies, desperately trying to link a Clinton is Good D/A. Therefore, when confronted with an affirmative on which he has a thick file of handbook evidence taking up space in his sixth tub, the 1N will run the same tired arguments that everyone else runs — and is your meat.

Don't think so? Imagine what the 2N will say to the 1N after the debate if they lose and the 1N refused to run the canned arguments. Oh no, peer pressure demands that the 1N start reading and stop thinking.

But of course, you can read handbooks, too. Therefore you KNOW every argument that your opponent will read.

The well-dressed 1AR begins with...

The Cross-ex of the 1NC

2. Use the cross-ex of the 1N to force the negative to take a position. If the negative is supporting the status quo, make them say it. If it's a counterplan, explore the values behind the counterplan. This is critical to setting up turns to disadvantages; if you can do something valuable better than the negative can, you win.

3. Use the cross-ex to tidy up the flow sheet. NEVER believe the judge who claims he/she/it can flow anything. Make sure that the area, that you believe will make you mileage, is well identified.

4. Use your prep time before the cross-ex, not after it. There are so many good reasons for this that the practice of leaping up for the cross-ex is incomprehensible. You NEED the time to get your act together — use it.

The 2nd Affirmative Constructive

5. Turn disads. Don't mess up the flow sheet with poor turns. But a good turn puts the burden of the negative strategy back onto the negative- miss a turn, and they lose.

6. Apportion your time well. If you cover everything completely in this speech, so much more the pressure on the 2NR. (Yes, that's right.)

7. Read the critical evidence into the round NOW. You KNOW what the 2N will say — anticipate it and get the evidence into the round NOW.

8. Establish decision rules that will help you turn the disads, or choose to ignore them. This is the true meaning of impacting an argument, and everything you say in the 2AC should impact the round.

The Cross-ex of the 2nd Negative

9. This is key to the 1AR; you MUST clean up the flow sheet so that signposting has been reinforced for the judge. Once again, do not believe the judge who says he can flow anything. In the heat of the 1AR, all it takes is a shaky signpost and that judge is lost for one argument or for several. And guess who gets the blame?

10. On each point that you plan to assault, establish a label; "so sub B is nuclear war, right?" As these labels are established, the 1AR SHOULD BE WRITING THEM DOWN. Otherwise the 1AR won't remember them, and thus the process of labeling is a waste. I try to get my debaters to use a steno pad, one argument per page; but since no one else does it this way, they go ahead and use the legal pad system and get lost on the flow like everybody else. Que sera sera.

11. After the mess has been cleared up, shut up and sit down. This cross-ex is prep time for the 1NR.

The First Affirmative Rebuttal

The 1st Affirmative Rebuttal

12. Begin with a canned statement that you have practiced, so you can get your adrenaline under control. Otherwise, you will stumble and begin to panic. The moment of beginning the 1AR is the most charged moment in a debate — everyone knows that the round depends on this speech. That is why you need a clear pathway to begin. Try something like, "the negative has never proven to you why China should be allowed to violate human rights with impunity", or a blanket statement like; "I will use the labels established in cross-ex to identify the plan attacks."

13. Cover the 2NC first. If you drop any of the 2NC's arguments, you can be sure that it will appear in the 2NR. A dropped argument from the 1NR has to first go through the process of the 2N understanding it before it can hurt you!

14. On each argument, give the label from the cross-ex, say how many responses you will have, give them, and then GO ON! Time spent identifying arguments, or explaining your responses, is all wasted. Your job is to make ink flow!

15. Say each response slowly, and say it only once. I guarantee you that you can cover more ground slowly than you can at hyperspeed. The reason is simple — you repeat yourself at hyperspeed.

16. Do the same on case; avoid explaining and babbling.

17. You will then find yourself with the greatest reward that a 1AR can experience - time to go back over the debate and show what the negative dropped. This leads to a beautiful sight — the 2N turning and glaring at the lower life form called "partner"; "Well, you couldn't even keep him busy, could you?" Almost all 2N's will drop case if it is covered in the 1AR, and this means the affirmative will win, even if some disads are iffy.

It's like this — a poor 1AR is fifty per cent the fault of the second affirmative. And only by practice and consistency can the 1AR become a consistent well-dressed performance.

But I can promise you this; if the first affirmative can reach that consistency and lay a carpet of ink, and if by the end of the 1AR the debate is TIED, then the affirmative has won the debate.

The Second Negative Rebuttal
or
Cell!
(originally published November 1989, revised July 1995)

"O.K. wimp. Welcome to cellblock B! You see yer cellmates — Moe, Flo, and Day-Glo. We been waitin' fer you. What's a li'l bitty mite like you servin' time fer in the Big House?"

"Lying in the last rebuttal."

"Mite, we all done horrible things. Moe held up banks in three states. Flo tore tags off mattresses. Day-glo sniffed paint. But none of us *ever* stooped so low as to get caught prevaricatin' in the last rebuttal"

"Just a li'l fib or two. Everyone does it."

"Oh, yer right about that, kid. Doan make it right, though.."

"Strange. That's what the judge said. Got away with it for most part of three years. But I got caught. It musta been somethin' the second negative did."

"You got caught redhanded? What did that negatory speaker say?"

"Well, the judge gave me an article about it fer me to study. Lord knows I have plenty of time to learn how to read it. Here it is."

The Grease Cutter

Dear Second Negative Rebuttalist —
You have four, or maybe five, minutes to stop the show and inoculate the judge against the Big Affirmative Lie. Too many 2NR's fail to perform three vital functions of the last rebuttal:

1. Pull through and impact the 1NR.

2. Give the judge something to vote for when the critic decides to vote negative.

3. Give reasons to ignore the affirmative's last lie.

Each of these functions have their roots earlier in the debate.

The First Negative's Arguments in the 2NR

How many times have you seen the 2NR punt his colleague's arguments? As a result, case side is often entirely ignored in the last negative rebuttal. Unfortunately, 2AR's usually figure out that the best part of the affirmative position has been dropped, and they usually mention it to the judge — for about three minutes.

At the same time, the strategy of the first negative merely tossing out a few arguments and waiting for the affirmative to mishandle them (maybe) is just a gift to the competent affirmative. For a true division of labor, the first negative rebuttal should say something that can win the debate.

But 1Ns often give up on their partners, thinking that they will be ignored in the last rebuttal. So they get up and try to answer everything that the 2AC said in eight minutes. This loses both the 2N and the judge, and the first negative has to hope the 1AR blows it so he can at least get the three ranking!

But as usual, this is the 1N's fault. A wise 1NR pulls through just enough arguments to meet two criteria that:

A. force the 1AR to have to spend serious time to answer them properly and

B. are simple for the 2N to understand, so they won't be butchered in the rebuttal.

This is possible, but only with a change of mindset.

1. Each argument must be carefully delivered. It should include a signpost, a minimum number of responses (five or six responses in 1NR just cries out for the 2N to drop the argument if the 1AR gives responses in return even if she/he groups them), evidence, and an impact. The first and last steps are the most crucial. The signpost is for your Beloved Pard, who is still over there meditating the brilliance of nuke war D/As. The impact is for the judge, because the 2NR will almost never give the correct one. Instead, 2A will grab your argument and impact it with one of his other D/A's!

   By impact I mean why the judge should vote on that argument alone. Again, that doesn't mean you have to blow up the world to get the vote, even for de College Judge. 1NR is a good place to read theory evidence, because it forces the 1AR to read evidence back, and those cards are *never* short.

2. The prep time before the 1AR is a perfect time to seize your partner's hair and bang his head viciously into the desk. Then, sweetly ask him to tell you what you said in your speech. Then, when he stares blankly, sink your pen into the fleshy part of his thigh. The resulting blood might bring a sympathy vote for the judge, and (seriously) next time maybe he'll remember to listen and write down what you said. The 2N should be writing continually during your rebuttal, and should be able to tell you exactly what the arguments were and what the impacts were.

3. Listen to the 1AR and flow it. Then YOU decide what should be pulled through in the last rebuttal. Remember, the 2NR has a window of about a minute and a half in the last speech for you. You deserve that time, but demanding more, exalts your arguments too much — by the end of the 1AR you have had ample time to win them clearly. Drop anything else, particularly anything that forces the 2NR to explain.

4. Before the 2NR, you tell your Pard what you want pulled through, and then get out of the his face. Turn away and sacrifice a quote to the gods, but let the 2NR work!

The Second Negative Rebuttal or Cell!

The Structure of the 2NR

5. The 2NR's first argument should try to seal the ballot. If you can get the judge to reach for the ballot then, it doesn't really matter what else you and the 2AR say, now does it? Therefore pick whatever argument, wherever it is, that will win the debate.

6. Then go to your colleague's arguments. This is a courtesy to her, and by golly she will be sitting next to you for the next couple of days, so you had better cover what she thinks is critical to survive the weekend. Spend one and one half minutes, more only, if you are getting your plow cleaned on plan.

7. Pull through only the arguments you clearly win on plan. You have two minutes in a four-minute rebuttal, and three minutes in a five-minute rebuttal to pull through the cream of your arguments. That is all. Unless you want to get slimed. If you don't, then you must practice Inoculation.

8. Inoculation is a challenge to the affirmative that also writes the ballot for the judge. Put down your notes. The judge looks up. Your eyes meet. For the first time in the debate, someone is actually going to communicate. The judge feels the pitter-patter of that last cuppa from the lounge. You speak:

    "In the next speech, please make the affirmative answer five arguments 1,2,3,4,and 5 (from memory). If she can do that, then please go ahead and adopt the affirmative policy. But if she cannot, you have good reason to vote negative in this debate."

9. Judges love inoculation. It sounds fair. And it keeps them listening for the answer to those arguments, rather then the Crisco that the 2AR would rather talk about.

10. If the 1AR dropped a large number of arguments, merely change the speech to:

    "We have been demanding answers to X arguments in this

debate. The affirmative has never talked about them. We believe that these arguments alone are enough to justify a negative ballot. If the affirmative chooses to finally answer them in this this last speech, they obviously feel so, too. Please vote negative."

11. But what if you challenge the 2AR to answer the arguments and she does? You lose. But, buddy, if you were in such bad shape going into the last speech that you would lose when the affirmative chooses to answer you *on your ground*, you were doomed anyway.

12. But what if you have to get through that last D/A? Listen, friend. Nothing is more important that forcing the 2AR to deal with your arguments. The preceding 3 and $^1/_2$ minutes should have contained more than enough to win the debate. But if you don't inoculate, you will probably lose anyway. Overtime is too late.

"Pretty interesting, mite. You gonna do this stuff when you get sprung on parole?"

"What? And actually have to debate? Why should I? No one actually does this stuff!"

"Well, Boys, there goes the neighborhood. Next thing ya know, they'll give us somebody who gives canned extemps."

In a Clearing Stands a Boxes
(Forgive me, Shakespeare and Paul Simon)

We join Julius Caesar as he prepares to go to the Senate.

Julie: Dang it, wife! Less starch in the togas! These wrinkles are as sharp as a knife!

Calpurnia: Oh, that reminds me. I had a dream!

Julie: By the way you snored, I bet it was about chain saws.

Calpurnia: Well, there was a massacre involved...

Julie: Look, I don't have time for this Lincoln–Douglas touchy-feely type stuff. Where did I put that decree?

Calpurnia: Oh, honey. Do you really think policy debate needs a set of laws?

Julie: Wife, we've gone over this before. There's a desperate need. The activity is out of control. Cicero himself couldn't pick up a speaker point in some of these spew rounds. It's time to put persuasion back in the activity.

Calpurnia: What are you, emperor or something? No one can decree persuasion!

Julie: Well-

Calpurnia: Aw, cmon, honey. Listen to your old debate opponent. How did we meet?

Julie: You know I remember very well...

Calpurnia: Tell me again.

In a Clearing Stands a Boxes

Julie: (sighs) It was the third round at the Hercules Tournament of Champions...

Calpurnia: And who was affirmative?

Julie: You were.

Calpurnia: And who was negative?

Julie: I was.

Calpurnia: And the resolution was...

Julie: Resolved: that the Republic should significantly change its foreign policy towards the Kingdom of China.

Calpurnia: Amazing how things stay the same! And how many disadvantages did your fine team from Romulus Remus Memorial High run?

Julie: Just XXVIII!

Calpurnia: That's all? And did it work?

Julie: The judge was stupid! That Fabius! You gotta remember, he's the one that got trampled by the elephant—

Calpurnia: Yes. I thought I won. Didn't you ever wonder why?

Julie: Now that you mention it, I saw you and Fabius...

Calpurnia: Never mind what you saw. I boxed you.

Julie: What?

Calpurnia: It's a technique that I learned from that adorable Crassus Riffer. It's guaranteed to beat the spew.

Julie: Well, I'll have that pencil necked Greek fed to the lions!

Calpurnia: Listen to me. You remember how my colleague, Cleo, used to go into those stream of unconsciousness multiple responses? Some of them were jewels, and others were as ridiculous as what that soothsayer told you yesterday.

Julie: Ides of March — absurd!

Calpurnia: Readjust the toupee, sweetie. Spare Riffer for me, and listen to what he says. When your partner throws out the arguments, flow them all, but draw a box about the most important ones — the pearls and the rubies. Leave the fool's gold for the negative to worry about.

Julie: So?

Calpurnia: Then, when the crunch hits in the 1AR, focus only on the boxed responses. Drop the others, unless somehow they have been turned into an impact. There is no impact to losing a moot argument. Point out how the boxed responses still stand, and the debate becomes clear to the judge. And by the 2AR, he'll be lending you his ears.

Julie: Yeah, and knowing you two, other things. But why not just run only responses that could be boxed in the first place?

Calpurnia: Darling! That wouldn't be fashionable. Did you want Cleo to make an asp of herself? It just isn't done.

Julie: Hrrmph! I'll still strike off that Geek's, I mean Greek's head. Now, before I go, what about this dream?

Calpurnia: Forget it. Go to the Senate, all right? And don't forget to ask Brutus how many hamburgers he wants at our barbecue this weekend.

Julie: Oh, I can already tell you. He eats two.

Colleague Calamity

(originally published December, 1992. Revised July 1995)

O.K. So us psychiatrists get a bum rap. Everyone thinks we are a bunch of wimps with pointy beards who smile and nod a lot and ask you questions about beating your mother with a dead fish. By no means are we like that.

I don't even have a beard.

Maybe that's why I'm different. I'm a forensics shrink.

Yeah, that's right. I deal with those hard cases. The debaters with the meglomania complexes. The prima donna Dramatic Interps. The H.I.'s. Nuff said.

So I wasn't surprised when I got a message on my car phone that another kid had flipped out over in the 'burbs'. I pulled up in front of the house, and I knew that I had a case that could write a thousand doctoral thesi. In front of the house was a wooden booth with a chain saw mounted on a sign. "Homeless Dental Clinic" it read.

I knocked on the door and a nervous looking woman answered. I flashed her my diploma. "Thank God you're here!" she hollered, clutching my arm and leading me down into the basement. That is where I entered policy debate hell.

Papers everywhere. Paper hung on the wall by friction. Paper covering every inch of the floor. An entire rain forest in front of me. It was enough to make me vote for a growth disad.

And underneath the multicolored mess, a body stirred. I tried to get to it, but I stumbled over Malthus and Cuban-Angolan Intervention. I had heard that these arguments were slippery, but I had never believed it until now.

Yes, there was a young girl under all the papyrus. An eyeball, shedding salt water like bad plumbing in a submarine, looked at me with desperation. A sound surfaced from under a post-it note. "Have you seen him?" the sound said.

Instantly I knew the problem. I had seen it a thousand times. I knelt on Malthus and spoke. "Colleague difficulty, huh? Can't get your partner to do his fair share of the work?"

She surfaced and sneered at me. She would be a toughie, all right. "What makes you think that, White Coat?"

I wouldn't let her get next to my skin like that. It cost me a good twelve thousand bucks of tuition to get to wear that lab coat. "Classic case. Here you are, obviously distraught. Tons of work to do, right? No help, right? So you blame old El Partnero, Tonto, Kemosabi and all that. Am I right?

I knew I had her on the run, so when she opened her mouth I plunged on. After all, this was my cross-ex.

"And your mother is very upset. Don't you care about that?" My professional training told me that hadn't struck home. It was in the way she laughed. Resistance. I had seen it a thousand times. So I gave her a grin and went on.

"You're lucky I stopped by. Here, look at this." I pulled out my scholarly article on Colleague Abuse, and tossed in to her. It raised a lump on her head.

"Ow! You think I have time to read this? Summarize it for me!"

So I did.

THE FORENSICS SHRINK'S TEN COMMANDMENTS OF COLLEAGUE COMMUNICATION.

1. Treat your colleagues as you would like to be treated. Like do you enjoy debating by yourself? Then why not a mutual wake-up pact? And why is it the five-three girl in spike heels carries the files while the six foot goon manhandles the flow pads? Huh? Natural selection?

II. Refer to your team in the Royal We; for example "We broke at Waw-Waw High; We made the cover of the Rostrum in the special anthropology issue."

III. Walk away from conversations about your colleague behind his/her/its back. No matter how much fun it may be to stick in the knife, it'll cut your back sooner or later.

IV. Plan out your work schedule with your partner at the beginning of each week, and then live by it. And take care of your part of the team. Why are you going to the double overtime football game before the Saturday tournament, while your colleague gets the eight hours of sack? You a poster child for Caffeine Anonymous? What's fair about it?

V. Never plan to go to another tournament without your partner unless he/she/it is happy about it. You may enjoy your vacation, but the team will be dead when you're back.

VI. Never talk in the colleague's ear. Especially after a quick lunch at Taco Pedro's.

VII. The First Negative Gets To Talk First. This means that the Second Negative Has To Talk Second. The First Negative Calls the Tune. At the very least, the Second Negative Needs to Hum Along.

VIII. Never read ballots out loud. All you can do is hurt somebody's feelings. I'm sure it is very urgent that the whole bus knows that you got better ranks than the creep you obviously dragged through the tournament.

IX. Talk. Rumor has it you both speak the same language. When you are having difficulties, it makes sense to talk to the fool before you call her one behind her back.

X. Never forget; they may give out speaker awards, but only one trophy per team. Think about it.

Colleague Calamity

I looked at her triumphantly. Her words began slowly.

"Great. Very wise. Wonderful. But you've made one mistake."

"I doubt it, but go on."

Suddenly she rent her garment. "I'm Seymour's girlfriend! He's disappeared in this mess! Help me find him!"

We did. He hadn't been dead that long.

Natty Bumppo's Debate Advice

(Originally published 1994)

And now, Natty Bumppo's advice for the debate-lorn.

(Dear Nat —)

(That's Mr. Bumppo to you.)

(Yeah. Right. I'm the first negative and the first affirmative, see? And I get the lower ratings every single time. And, like, it's no fair because I tell the jerk everything to say! But because he goes last, and gets to blow up the world, or save the world, or flip the judge's stomach, he gets all the credit. What can I do? Signed, Low-ranked in Lubbock)

Dear Lowball: Yours is a common problem. It is primarily the fault of human nature, namely that whoever goes last is in the judge's mind when it comes to ballot signing time. It also is human nature to believe that your contributions outweigh your partner. In other words, maybe he IS better than you are.

But, you wanted advice, not criticism. Some thoughts on the first negative rebuttal:

1. Remember this speech is critical for two people in the room. One is the judge. The other is your colleague. She may be a bum, but even a bum needs to understand an argument before she can give it. Therefore;

2. Signpost diligently. Your beloved pard has just sat down after eleven minutes on her feet. She will be less than fresh. You have to give her the break of clear signposting. To say "go to three" doesn't make much sense in the best of times, and this ain't one of them.

3. Impact slowly. Your 2NR should be able to flow it, too.

4. Pick and choose arguments. If you try to pull everything, you are merely postponing the decision of what to drop for the 2NR, and that person is not as committed to the arguments as you are.

(You probably didn't understand that, because you are too committed to the spread 'em technique of overburdening the 1AR. I realize its the fashion, but its also the reason you are getting the lousy ranks. You really aren't playing a critical role in the debate — why should you get better ranks than the fellow who is?)

(Dear Mr. Bump: I ran up against a killer bee affirmative at my last debate. I tried to run logical arguments against the case, but all the judge would allow me to say was topicality without evidence. Has debate sunk so low? Signed, Evidenceless in Evansville)

Frankly, Ev, one of the real irritations of judging high school policy rounds is the failure of 1NCs to run anything but that he/she/it is programmed to run. Once again, that may be the current style, or strategy, but a friend of the 1N it is not.

So, how about this?

1NC observation on quality of evidence

A. A critical dimension of debate is the quality, specifically the relevance, of evidence read into a round.

   1. A policymaker would never choose a new policy based on irrelevant events.

   2. The theory of prima facie insists that an affirmative be supported with critical evidence before it can be evaluated.

   3. The test of a piece of evidence is whether it is specifically related to the claim.

B. This affirmative's evidence is incredible, in every sense of the word.

1. The solvency evidence is irrelevant to the plan.
2. Without solvency evidence, no affirmative should be debated.

C. Reject the affirmative as not prima facie. As soon as they try to read solvency evidence, realize that it is a tacit admission that the case was not prima facie, and vote!

D. Even if you don't believe this, please apply the standard as soon as the affirmative begins attacking our lack of evidence, as they must agree with the test.

Then, run some logical argument, and bait the affirmative into the no evidence response. Notice that the argument insists that a policymaker pay attention to it. Notice further that it can be adapted to a tabula rasa or a storytelling paradigm.

Will a judge like it? Well, you have nothing to lose but the loss.

(Dear Gnat: I love cross-ex, but some judges go out and smoke during it. This somewhat dampens my enthusiasm. What should I do? Signed, Second Hand in Seattle)

Dear Sea: Well, that all depends on whether you want to win the debate or not. Here's what I'd say as the next speech starts. But then, I don't have to win any debates anymore.

Observation: You should disqualify yourself as an incompetent judge.

A. Debate is a rational activity. It's roots are Platonic, and it's effects are widespread and lasting, such as your decision to stop smoking and come back in to listen to it.

B. You are irrational.

   1. You walked out on the most critical part of the debate, namely the cross-ex.

Natty Bumppo's Debate Advice

      a. Cross-ex is critical to understanding argument. (read ev.)
      b. Cross-ex is a source of stasis, which identifies the positions of each team. (read ev.)

   2. Further, you walked out to smoke, which is not only irrational, but disgusting. (see the Surgeon General)

C. You have only two options

   1. Resign, and we'll go get a competent judge.

   2. Vote for US, in recognition of the error of your ways.

D. Pre-empt. Unless the other side reads evidence denying the critical nature of cross-ex, any decision in their favor is active proof of your incompetence. NO paradigm possibly allows any other decision.

Thank you.

(Natt, you jerk. I smoke. I know where you live! Signed, Arnold in Atlanta.)

(That's all the time we have for now. Au revoir. And send my mail courtesy of the Witness Protection Program.)

Division of Labor? Sounds Like Work to Me

(originally published January 1989, revised beyond recognition June 1995)

It was a romantic evening. The moon shone through the windows, and the whispers (well, the screams) from the other rooms faded as I looked into her eyes. I could have sworn that that the good one winked at me. She was at that instant, blind with love. I knew — I knew I was hers.

She rose and walked toward me. The two thousand briefs in her hand crackled in the hiss of the steamy heat.

Once again her eye smiled, her foam flecked lips parted, and she nuked my crummy first negative.

As my "nuclear winter" lost to her "proliferation is good" canned brief, I began to wonder.

"Who thought up this crummy division of labor business anyway?"

O.K., maybe you wouldn't think that, but consider - the division of labor is supposed to be strategic. It should do three things;

   a. keep the negative on the same course, without needlessly duplicating arguments,

   b. put the most pressure on the affirmative, and

   c. win the debate, no matter who is the judge.

Yet the most common versions of the division of labor — the Traditional and the Shell Game, fail to do all of the above.

Failure of the Traditional Model

The Traditional Model divides the affirmative into case and plan. The first negative is given the case arguments, which are significance, harm, inherency, and for the brain dead, topicality. Yet all but the last of these have fallen into disrepute, and the last one is only popular because it is the refuge of the lazy.

Consider inherency. The problem is the lack of impact to the argument. It is not pre-emptive for most judges — that is, if you win inherency, you usually don't win the debate. Even the stock issues judge will not vote on inherency very often, because the esteemed critic will probably not agree that the issue you are attacking is inherency!

Further, the real world does not make decisions based on the first negative issues. I do not examine harm or significance before going to a movie, or even bigger decisions like, oh, getting married.

Therefore, keeping the REAL issues out of the debate until the second negative often looks like sandbagging. Even worse, it allows a slippery, fast 1AR to one-line the plan attacks out of the debate. The 2NR is not long enough to cut the Crisco.

When you are affirmative, what arguments do you think will beat you? Obviously, relevant solvency and disadvantages are the worst arguments, because when run well, they reflect the real world.

Flaws with the Shell Game

Yet the accepted system of the Shell Game is easy to beat. If you have a dinosaur for a coach (like me) and the concept is foreign to you, 1NC runs the shell, and the 2NC attempts to "blow it up". This is all the rage at debate camps, because it's easy to can up in the week before the tournament. It is also extremely easy to beat.

Oh, I can hear the howls already. Face reality, folks. The shell immediately is predictable, and only an unprepared 2AC punts on it. If you are running something really squirrelly, it even works the first time a good team hears it.

But after going home and thinking up ten turns to the disad, the technique leaves you with the argument YOU BROUGHT INTO THE ROUND beating you on ONE turn. And the 2AR has just the speech to do it — and it takes only ONE TURN. Any idiot can pull through one argument and win it in 2AR.

But you say, the debate is already over before the 2AR? Sez who? All the 1AR has to do is throw enough ink to muddy the waters, and then let the 2AR pick up the pieces when it's too late.

And if the shell game works so well, why do affirmatives win so many more debates than negatives?

Opportunity Cost

Therefore, let's take a look at the division of labor based upon only the two criteria we posed above. It's clear we want a system that makes both speakers equally able to win the debate, without giving so much leeway that they contradict.

We will begin with the most basic of economic principles — the opportunity cost. This means that whenever we make a decision to do something, we sacrifice everything else we could have done instead. If I go get a pizza, I give up hamburgers, tacos, sushi, plus anything else I could have done with that money and the time that I used to purchase and snarf the pizza. In debate terms, these costs fall into four areas; time, money, resources, and labor.

Let's take China. An affirmative proposes that we take away Most Favored Nation status because of human rights violations by the PRC. When we make this decision, we agree to forfeit at least the following:

Time: we have wasted all our efforts at reconciliation with the Chinese — we are back on square one. All the businesses that have attempted to enter the Chinese market will have wasted all their time in doing so plus impacts on the economy and world stability.

Money: as all those cheap clothes and plastic vomit become scarce, we will spend more for these necessities. That may sound flip(sorry) but Chinese products are obviously a choice of many because of their low prices. People will either have to shift to new preferences or pay more money. Impacts - economic inefficiency leads to recession, monopoly, and the dreaded trade wars.

Resources: we are coldbloodedly using China as a source of support for our military industrial complex. When we shut off the lucrative arms market, we must choose whether to: (1) sell the guns elsewhere (impact- north south), (2) buy the excess weapons ourselves to keep the MIC solvent (deficit d/a) or (3) let the MIC exit to other countries, turning us to a third rate power, and making Newt very unhappy.

Labor: besides the obvious implications in the arguments above, the China market is a major impetus behind keeping organized labor in check within the United States. This move will be seen as a victory for unions, with all the nasty implications for America that libertarians will be happy to doomsay you.

Here is my point, these are the arguments that affirmatives do NOT want to hear. Each one not only can beat the affirmative all by themselves, but they also support a common world view. That world view turns out to be that of the Status Quo. This is good, because any attempt to flip these arguments, runs into the most obvious of responses - where are the impacts in the SQ?

How do we make a framework to get these arguments into the debate early enough to keep from being slimed, yet late enough to give the 2NC something to do?

The New Division of Labor

Every affirmative should cover the issues of significance/harm, inherency, and usually solvency in the 1AC. Any 1AC that fails to do so should be badgered with prima facie argumentation. For the purposes of the formula, let's express the affirmative case as a plan, an advantage, and three subpoints. Sure, there are lots of ways to organize an affirmative, but the trick is to recognize the issue wherever the affirmative has decided to stick it.

Affirmative case	INC	1NR
Plan		
Advantage		
A. significance/harm	alternate causalities	solvency
B. inherency	defense of the SQ	disads
C. solvency	attack the evidence	decision rule
	attack on the implications of the aff case	disad

Let's give an example, based again on a China affirmative linking MFN and human rights:

1AC	1NC
Plan: MFN status linked to human rights	
Advantage Aff saves the world from barbarism	
A. the Chinese are violating human rights	
1. forced abortion	alternate causality — pressure for forced abortion comes from the people
2. suppressing democracy	alternate causality — Chinese people are uncomfortable with democracy
B. Current efforts are failing	
1. not forceful enough	China is not reasonable on human rights
2. Clinton is namby-pamby	danger of conflict if goes too far

Division of Labor? Sounds Like Work to Me

C. Aff solves!

    1. MFN status is critical to China   *[evidence does not link abortion to MFN*

    2. Chinese leaders are pragmatic   *[they will do what the people demand*

Underview — control of human rights is a measure of sovereignty

A. sovereignty critical
B. China is at critical mass
C. U.S. demands response
D. DILEMMA—
    1. chaos or
    2. conflict

Second negative constructive

    D/A critical mass
        A. Answers to 2AC attack on the underview
        B. Extension of impact
        C. Implications of the argument
            1. Aff MUST show a favorable response to the U.S. action, not just a "reasonable one"
            2. US policy must succeed or US loses sovereignty

    D/A One billion peasants
        A. answers to the 2AC attack on alternate causality
        B. dilemma — the Chinese peasant is critical to the affirmative proposal, or it is not
            1. Is critical — the aff is an internal contradiction — if the wishes of the people are important, then forced abortion should continue
            2. not critical — then what was all this democracy hooey?

Basically, the second negative can use the 2AC arguments as a basis for her own arguments, while leaving the original impacts for the 1NR to pursue.

But Does It Work?

Does this system meet our criteria? I think it does.

A. The negative presents a unified front in defense of the SQ, while it remains on the attack.

B. The pressure on the 1AR is overwhelming, because one liners will not sufficiently obfuscate the argument.

C. The division of labor strokes all types of judges, from the dinosaur to the college fiend. It recognizes issues, debates policy, and blows up the world.

I watched her walk back to her chair — the blood of my arguments still dripping from her lips. I waited for my opportunity — but at what cost?

I Love to Tell the Stories

(Originally published 1995)

"O.K., students, it's Storytime."

"Amy, get your head off the floor. Kevin, put back the computer."

Once upon a time, there was a beautiful but tragic damsel named Harm. She lived in a Border town with her many children, Significance. It was a hard life, filled with longing. She was oppressed by a dastardly villain, Inherency. Inherency loved to torture Harm, and made his nefarious presence known by many structures, attitudes, and gaps (in his teeth).

But one day, a handsome Solvency rode into town. He had a plan to free Harm and her children from the odious clutches of Inherency.

Of course, Inherency would not leave town without a fight. He spread all sorts of nasty lies, Disadvantages, about Solvency. But Harm saw the true beauty of Solvency, and they chased Inherency and his lies out of town.

"I love happy endings. Zach, stop that spray painting. I have another story. Just listen."

Once upon a time there lived in a small border town, a soiled dove named Inherency. She had lived a somewhat dissolute life, carrying on with politicians and other such loose folk. However, she was much more clever than people would give her credit for being, and it was through her clever reasoning that the town was basically prosperous. Her best friend, Harm, saw her true beauty, and even though the children of the town, all named Significance, were somewhat rowdy and liked to complain, they loved Inherency, too.

But then, a newspaper editor named Solvency moved to town. She spread all sorts of lies about Inherency, mostly playing to the ignorance of the populace. Solvency wanted to take over the town, and made all sorts of wild promises that nobody, particularly a sleaze like Solvency, could deliver. Inherency, of course, saw through all the cheap tactics, and saw the horrible Disadvantages that would occur if Solvency took over the town.

Standing up at the town meeting, Inherency presented the damaging knowledge of what she had discovered about Solvency, in a clear coherent speech, and Solvency was run out of town on a rail.

(Sigh.) "Very sweet. Ben, please don't play with explosives. Can you tell me what these stories mean?

"Yes, Georgia, it is very easy for novices to understand. The first story refers to the affirmative, and the second a narrative that the negative should tell. But, as brilliant as you are, there are lessons in these stories even for the fourth - year debaters.

"Have you heard about storytelling? Of course, it's the new fad on the circuit, right? Everyone talks about storytelling, and no one agrees what it means. A few years ago, the watchword was Impact. Everyone knew what that meant, too.

"Storytelling in debate should have the same elements as a story by Dr. Seuss. There should be a hero, a villain, both suitably motivated; there should be conflict, and the action should happen in sequence. Well…

"Affirmatives do this, sometimes by default, as they develop the 1AC. Unfortunately, as the trend continues for the negative to ignore case structure and to drag the affirmative off its ground with counterplans and critiques, affirmatives are dropping the narratives out of the opening presentation.

"The above mentioned trend by the negative, however, is the sign of a resurgence of storytelling on that side of the topic. For years, the claim of comparative advantage in the final rebuttal has punished negatives enough so that they have realized that the line by line responses alone no longer are effective.

"But negatives, in what stories they do tell, have fallen into a weak strategic position. The story now largely consists of a minor claim, (a disadvantage) which becomes developed into a War and Peace style epic. This strategy succeeds as long as the affirmative plays the game. But if the affirmative refuses to be dragged with the attack, and continues to push advantages, the final rebuttal remains critical. And then, naturally, when the negative gets the ballot back with an L, the judge is stupid.

(Sigh!) "Craig, keep your hands to yourself. Please remember the stories I told you above. Yes, I realize that it contains the dreaded "I" word, but it's not going to bite.

"Consider a case that the affirmative will often propose — exclusion of HIV infected immigrants. Let's consider what story the affirmative is likely to tell."

> *Who is Harm? Death.*
>
> *Who are her children, Significance? Oh, probably the entire human race, if the affirmative is up to the usual.*
>
> *Who is Inherency? Affirmatives claim that there is no policy to actively search for HIV, therefore a test needs to be applied to all immigrants.*
>
> *What is Solvency? The affirmative believes that an HIV test can adequately identify and exclude dastardly diseases.*

"I'm sorry, but that is shallow analysis. It's a weak story, based on scare tactics and the testimony of the Terminally Alarmed. Now, what will the negative story be?"

> *What is Inherency? Inherency refuses to sacrifice individual liberty to the AIDS scare. Harm is not nearly as alarming as Solvency makes her out to be. Treatments are being discovered, and a cure perhaps. But what is most important is the refusal of Inherency to violate rights, and the further refusal to insult foreign governments by declaring their citizens persona non grata.*
>
> *Further, Inherency recognizes that the affirmative increases the incentive toward illegal immigration, where the true dangers of infectious disease spread lie. Inherency recognizes alternate causalities of immigration, such as the desire to escape persecution, make it worth nearly any price to reach the Golden Shores. Therefore, increased restrictions leads to bigger disadvantages.*

I Love to Tell the Stories

Yet even now we are not finished. Solvency lied when she claimed she can detect HIV with a single test. Solvency lied when she asserted that fraud would play no role in the tests. And the presence of false positives makes the tragedy of her lies clearer.

"Now THAT, Josh, is a story."

"Say what? How do you run this in a round? You say you'll sound silly talking about heroes and villains? Well, if that bothers you (it doesn't me), find the appropriate terminology. But here is where the argumentation is applied. . ."

First negative constructive

Aff case	negative story (argument)
significance/harm	Solvency misanalyzed
	alternate causality
	diminish significance
	diminish harm
	or depending on the story, grant it!
inherency	here is why Inherency does what she does
	case specific d/a's
	generic d/a's
solvency	solvency lied
	plan meet advantage
	workability

Second negative constructive

significance/harm	answer responses, develop impact,
generally	solvency
inherency	answer responses, balloon
solvency	impact the solvency argument

First negative rebuttal, Second negative rebuttal

Tell the story in full as developed by end of constructives. Pull through what the affirmative has dropped. Ignore those parts of the affirmative that do not threaten your story. It is critical to keep and emphasize the narrative form. Challenge the affirmative to answer the story. Point how comparative advantage is NOT an appropriate response.

"Now, what about the affirmative?"

1. 1AC should emphasize the narrative. A thesis should appear early in the speech to make the major characters clear. An explanation of how the plan works and compares with Inherency is critical.

2. Transitions should emphasize the narrative. Substructure should make narrative clear. I think it is a rare set of evidence, combined with a rare speaker, that can make a story clear without some rhetoric.

3. If the negative tries to drag you away from your story, refuse to abandon your version. Find the weakness in the negative story, and concentrate on taking it out. The more complicated your responses become, the thicker the fog that obscures your strengths.

"And cross-ex?"

1. Use cross-ex to declare the major players in the narrative. Examine critical testimony in the light of the story the evidence must therefore tell. Find out how the expert witnesses do not agree with the story told by the opposition.

2. Establish a value system that re-inforces Harm or Disadvantages in your story. (I never seem to see this; maybe because it requires teamwork?)

"Yes, Megan? Topicality? That's who tells the story!"

"Now, I will read you my personal favorite, *Where the Wild Things Are*."

I Love to Tell the Stories

Individual Events

The Fundamentals of Interp
or
Golf and 'Night, Mother

(published 1996)

It all started with my friend, who has a duckhook.

No, he is not physically challenged. He can't seem to hit a golf ball without it making an extreme left turn. No turn signals, just straight for twenty yards and then whoosh, out of bounds.

And he tried to solve this by tinkering with his swing. He would concentrate on the address of the ball, and the takeaway, and the teachings of martial arts specialists in Thailand. Nothing worked.

Last weekend, he gave up, and went to the golf equivalent of the Betty Ford Clinic. They broke his swing apart and put it back together again. He is supposed to practice on the range every day for a month before he sets a limb back on the course again. He's crazy enough about golf; he might do it, too.

I found myself nodding my head as he told me about the approach that his pro had taken on his Lost Weekend. I almost went to sleep, before I suddenly realized with a jerk (no, he's not that bad) that the Aristotelian approach that the pro had used was very much like my own.

Aristotelean, in the distorted sense that I learned it, involves breaking an act into its fundamental parts, and then putting it back together again, completely corrected, step by step, until you approached perfection. It may not be everyone's philosophy, but it's mine, and I have some evidence for its efficacy.

No doubt you have suffered from blank ballot syndrome. This is a slump where you seem to be doing everything right, and you still can't grab any hardware. In Interp, it's a 3-3-5. In L–D, it's 2-2. In extemp, it's a 2-3-6. You get the idea.

So you grab the ballots to see what you are doing "wrong," and there's no answer. The ballots rave about your analysis, or your eye contact, or even your tie, and send you off with the three. What's the matter with these judges?

Nothing, buddy. You are in Mediocrity Land, and what the judge is trying to tell you is the equivalent of your ex-sweetie saying "you're nice, and I still want us to be friends."

So after nearly two decades of living on the public dole, I decided to set off in quest of the Fundamentals. The Right Stuff. The Answer to the Blank Ballot.

Interp — The Fundamentals

There are four: Face, Body, Voice and Purpose.

1. Face

I had a college theater prof who used to get so disgusted with our amateurish faces that he would scream "work your face! At least wink, or something! You're afraid your cheeks will crack?" It is often the same with you, my friend.

A. Your face should be different with every character. The eyes, especially, should show the different light that dwells within. The mouth should show the tension of each character. The eyebrows should move from character to character, and should move within the character's speech. As a test, perform in front of the mirror and only watch your eyes and eyebrows. What do you see?

B. In pauses, it is your face that carries the scene. In any pause in interp, the reason for the pause is for "something" to happen. That "something" is mainly expressed by the face.

C. The transition between characters on the face should be swift and not alarming. If you are becoming the "Elephant Man" in less that a tenth of a second, it is not surprising that the judge is distracted by your gyrations. What is "big" is not necessarily effective. Less exaggeration might be better.

2. Body

A. If a ruler could balance on your shoulder in the transition between characters, you are probably boring.

B. If the judge can look at your belly button and never have to move her eyes, you are probably boring. You should also buy some appropriate clothes.

C. If the judge can dot an "i" and still see your character change, you are too slow.

D. If your gestures resemble chopping bread, you should try debate.

E. Your gestures should fit the mood of the moment, and fit the character. This seems obvious, but equally obvious is the fact that most interpers are not in control of their gestures. Every character has the same gestures!? This is unlikely in real life, don't you think?

3. Voice

Personally, I am more impressed with a well controlled voice than with a magnificent use of body and face. Maybe it's my five years in radio, but I find that most characters I judge are very flat in voice. Women doing males make their voices artificially deep and out of control. Men think female voices are high and whiny — extremely irritating! Yes, there are women who sound like that, but to think every woman does is misogyny (oh, go ahead and look it up).

A. It doesn't matter how high or low the character's voice may be- it's consistency that counts.

The Fundamentals of Interp

B. Very few voices should speak in social tones — the characters in a DI or HI are usually in situations that are far beyond that. It rings false when a character suddenly screams when previously talking in a social tone, no matter how loud.

C. Never chose a voice with which you cannot express the full range of emotion — even if the character does not require it. You've chosen a "freak" voice, and the judge will listen to the voice, not the character.

D. Ideally, after tape recording your performance, a listener should not recognize any voice on the tape excepting one. That is the ideal. But a harsher test, and more a test predicting success, is that the listener becomes caught up in the story and forgets which voice is the interper's.

4. Purpose

For a much better and extensive dissertation, consult the first six lessons of *Acting One* by Robert Cohen. The four components of Purpose go by the acronym VOTE. It is a magnificent system because anytime in the interp the character can be analyzed as to his/her VOTE. If the interper can't tell the vote, then the performance must by definition be flat.

A. Every character must have a goal towards which he/she is struggling. Every speech must reflect this "Victory." If a speech does not, then it's worse than irrelevant — it bores and distracts.

B. Every character must have a clearly recognized "Obstacle" that he/she sees as getting in the way of "Victory." When that character appears, his/her obstacle should clearly be seen in the eyes, body and voice.

C. Every character has a plan to follow in overcoming the "Obstacle" and achieving "Victory." This is a conscious decision called "Tactics" — here is how "I" will win. Then every speech is moving towards winning. This gives an urgency to the character that makes the scene move.

D. Every character has an "Expectation" of how the "Tactics" will work. The character either believes he/she will succeed, or believes that the effort will probably be futile. This colors the lines in a way that makes the scene come alive. A correct choice of "Expectations" creates reality. A bad choice makes the scene ring false, and gives you that magnificent three ranking.

Consider this as your goal — if you do all the above well, you CANNOT fail at making an impression on the judge. And at the least, the critic will be able to tell you exactly why you received the ranking you did. And then, if the ballot is blank, you can assume the worst; "if you can't say anything nice, don't say anything at all."

Too Dumb To Breathe
(published 1995)

You notice the back of the room is going to sleep?

You ask "Can everyone hear me?" and a guy on the front row says "What?"

Are people in the closest rows turning around to explain what you said to the people behind them? Do they then laugh?

Maybe you need some help.

Perhaps the help you need is with your voice. You don't have proper breath support. You aren't enunciating your words properly. You, my friend, are a mess.

Let's take a look at the voice, which may seem to be contradictory. Let's begin with a rough diagnosis.

Go into your bathroom, and lock the door. Ignore the people who soon will be pounding on it, demanding to know what you are doing in there.

Imagine you are the star in an opera. You have lost your one true love, and have decided to end it all by hanging yourself. It's a huge concert hall, and the mikes are all out, and its a benefit performance for the Terminally Hard of Hearing.

Now sing.

Uh-uh. Not loud enough.

L-O-U-D-E-R! That's better.

Now, place your fingers lightly on your throat, and pump up the volume even more. If you feel a tightening under your fingers, relax, and use your stomach to pump out the sound.

Stop. How do you feel? There are several answers.

1. I feel pretty stupid. So? If this is your only problem, feel lucky.

2. I'm exhausted. This means you are lacking in proper breath support. As we'll see in just a moment, it's a correctable problem, but it is causing your voice to die about row five.

3. I'm dizzy. You have major breath support problems. They are affecting not only your voice, but your health in general.

4. My throat hurts. You weren't singing louder. You were screaming. Once again you need to gain breath support.

Armed with your diagnosis, let's work on a prescription.

The voice begins with support from the diaphragm. This a powerful muscle extending underneath your lungs, and its job is to pump air. When used properly, the stomach should rise and fall, not the chest.

A. Lay down. Put one hand on your chest and the other on your stomach. Breathe so that the hand on your stomach rises and falls, and the hand on your chest remains still. Notice a couple of things; first, you don't have to breathe as often, and second, that you get a rush of oxygen that makes you dizzy — more symptoms of inadequate breath support.

B. Now, of all the exercises in the world, here is one of the most pleasurable. Practice breathing as you go to sleep — it will reinforce the new behavior, and it will give you pleasant dreams!

Next, move up the body to your throat. Massage the area around the larynx. Stop if it feels too good. Just kiddin'. Now hum a little. Feel the voice box tense up or relax depending on the volume and effort you are expending. The key here is to relax.

Easy to say, and hard to do? Of course. But consider a couple of facts. The phone company did a series of surveys to determine what type of voice that Americans found to be most pleasant. The answer was clear, voices in the lower register of both the male and female range. There isn't much you can do about the pitch that your parents granted you, besides taking various steroids and other nasty substances. But, the more you relax your throat, the lower your voice, and also the less likely you will choke or stumble. A few exercises to start you on the way.

C. Visualization. There is a drop of green liquid on your fingertip. Touch your throat. The green liquid spreads, relaxing your muscles around the larynx. Practice this and a touch right before you speak will trigger the relaxation.

D. For the visually inclined; take a piece of paper. Blow across it to make it vibrate. That is how your vocal cords work. Now crumple op the paper — gee, it doesn't work anymore. Plant that picture in your mind, right next to Marsha Brady freezing up in the school assembly.

Now back to what you can do something about — the holes in your head. Yes, even you have them — the nasal cavities. You are reminded of them every time you have a cold, and you suddenly sound like Porky Pig. The nasal passages vibrate to give a quality to the voice called resonance, a vibration that most people, and the phone company, finds very attractive. It is why Woody Allen makes the claim that Americans will follow any leader with a well-modulated voice.

The opposite of resonance, however, is a very obnoxious quality called nasality, literally talking through your nose. This is what will drive your audience up and out of their seats.

E. Hold your nose between your index and thumb. Put it just below the tough cartilage and just rest your fingers there. Now, say the Pledge of Allegiance (Don't let anyone see you who may think this is a political statement). Three results are possible:

1. You feel nothing. Call your attorney. You are deceased.

2. Your fingers feel a vibration on a few sounds, and not others. Congratulations! You cannot help but make some sounds with the assistance of your nose. Try NNNN... the tongue touches the

top of your mouth, and vibrates the nose. But on other sounds, there should be no vibration at all, and that is why...

    3. You feel constant vibration. Ouch! You are Porky Pig.

F. As in E, hold your nose and say the Pledge again. Do your best to NOT vibrate the nose, without drooling. Do it again. Notice you are actively lowering the focus of your energy to talk out your mouth. This is a habit, and it takes the same effort to break any other habit.

G. Put your fingers in your ears and do the Pledge again. That awful sound is your skull vibrating. It is also why tape recorders misfunction every time you speak into them. Yes, Matilda, that really is your voice. No, there is really nothing you can do except accept it.

The clincher is this — poor voices cost money. Correction in most cases is merely the changing of habit. Until they pass another amendment to the Civil Rights Act protecting people with sandpaper voices from discrimination, it's up to you to do something about it.

It's in the Bag

(Originally published 1994)

- Um, hi!

- 'Lo.

- Nice day, huh?

- I wouldn't know.

- No, I guess not. What with the paper bag and all.

- Oh. You noticed.

- Well, it is rather hard to miss.

- My coach made me do it. He says my acting has all the range of a sack. So I thought I'd wear this to prove him wrong.

- And?

- He hasn't noticed. But I did get a two last round.

- I'm sure that's progress. Listen, it isn't possible to correct anyone's acting disabilities in a single column. But here are some suggestions I ripped off from some excellent coaches, and two thought provoking books (see below). You might try out these ideas, and see if the paper sack isn't necessary any more.

I. Grab some James-Lange theory — this concept argues that our inner reactions often build as we take on outer expressions. This is the idea behind "wear a happy face and soon you will be." In short, act like it, and it soon will be true. This may be an approach that can break an interping rut wide open.

For example, you have a hysterical section in your D.I. (um, who DOESN'T have a hysterical...never mind). This section seems never to sell itself, to the judges or anyone else. This is probably because it has never been sold to the most important audience — you.

Get some privacy, and a mirror. Picture hysteria. Try it in the mirror. It will be awful. Try it until you can approach some clinical detachment in doing the exercise. If it helps, dim the lights so only your major features are visible. Otherwise that flaming zit will keep bringing you back to adolescent reality (unless it makes you hysterical then hey, whatever works...).

Keep working at it, until you can feel what it takes to appear hysterical. Then, like muscle memory in sports, duplicate the expression until you can reproduce it, even when you are not hysterical.

Now for most of us, this won't be enough to fool anyone in a round. But if it's good enough to fool YOU, then genuine emotions can follow.

II. Learn the tools of the trade — All actors (or interpers, if you insist) have three tools for expression: the face; the body; and the voice. All three of these tools works at various levels of intensity, much like an amplified speaker. Great emotion and impact can be generated at low volumes, but at the very top, overamplication can cause some wretched sound — and acting. Do some experimenting with small, very small, acting levels, and see what happens. Try this line at MAXIMUM intensity, Normal levels, and teeny tiny intensity.

"It doesn't matter. By this time tomorrow, we'll be dead anyway."

(Why this particular line? A couple of years ago, an interper set up four feet away from me, and screamed it in my face. It was a memorable experience.) I think that you will find the minimum treatment by far the most effective, even though most high school actors wouldn't play it that way.

III. Shake your body! — some basic principles of use of the body, particularly the hands and the arms.

   A. In general, positive emotions expand, and negative emotions contract. Get happy, get bigger. Grief — let's watch you slowly shrink. Playing the scene from *The Elephant Man*, as Merrick suffers rejection, the actor should start big and then get smaller, smaller, until by the end of the scene we feel as tiny as Merrick, and just as deformed. I've seen some amazing work with this principle, even though sometimes the interper didn't even recognize what she was doing.

   B. Most gestures should curve, not chop, unless the idea is to suggest nervousness or strong negative emotion. As a corrollary, most gestures should not cross the body, unless you intend something to really glare in the judge's eyes. For example in in *Little Big Man*, after the massacre at the Battle of the Washita, Jack Crabb might reach across his body to pick up some bloody water from the river, and fling it *across* his body away from him, suggesting the sign language for death. But as with all dramatic gestures, a very little is sometimes too much!

   C. Every character of substance has a "master gesture" that immediately identifies that character — the nervous brush of the hair, the flip-flop of a palm, the finger on the side of the nose (if you're playing Santa Claus). Generally, as with many theatre conventions, this follows a rule of three; the gesture increases in effectiveness to the third repetition, and decreases rapidly thereafter. So, look for a critical time for the third repetition — either as a way of identifying the character in a possibly confusing passage, or highly amplified at a peak moment.

   D. Business — characters need to be doing something. Many times the piece suggests appropriate "stuff," and sometimes it doesn't. Therefore, there are two types of business: "definite" which is necessary action such as answering doors and phones; and "indefinite," like the ubiquitous cigarette. Business makes a character much more real and increases the perceived difficulty of the piece.

It's in the Bag

IV. **In your face!** — I had a director in college who used to scream to us "Work your face!" This used to give us plenty of ammunition for imitating him behind his back. And it's true that unmotivated facial movement makes one look viciously depraved.

However, after years of chewing on half-baked and sometimes totally raw interpers, I can testify that the average high school actor underplays the face, particularly the lower jaw. Not only does this make the actress appear as if her chops are wired shut, it also reduces the quality of her direction.

Two other basic principles: react before you act; and show the reaction of characters who are listening to critical lines. Example — phone rings. Character who is going to answer the phone looks at the phone, then reaches for it. "Hello? Aunt Margaret! I thought you had fallen overboard into the school of sharks!" Cut over to Margaret's husband, even though he doesn't have the next line. Instead, his line is now business.

V. **Watch that tone of voice!** — Tones of voice come in four basic categories — domestic, social, business and solemn. An example of each; *domestic* — "I don't think I love you anymore;" *social* — "So I told him that I wanted a divorce;" *business* — "that divorce will be two thousand dollars, ma'am;" and *solemn* — "and that's why divorce lawyers drive Lamborghinis." Tones should change all the way through interps — it's the sure sign of a shallow interp when they don't! Listen to the conversation of your peers — hear the changes in tone? Note that some of the most shocking scenes in movies gain impact by the character delivering a critical line in the "wrong" tone. Of course, this only works if all the other lines are delivered in the right tone. (For all you Monty Python lovers; perhaps this is why their humor runs dry within a ten minute H.I.)

Most importantly, reconsider your script for its melody. Every script has a tune — it is the job of the interper to find the conjunction between his/her voice and the that tune. Consider the melody of *Greater Tuna* versus Woody Allen's "The Whore of Mensa." Both are very funny, and very wretched if delivered in the wrong tune.

Off the Subject
(Originally published 1995)

"Don't touch me! Don't try to stop me!"

"Whassa matter kid? You look upset."

"Good clue, Sherlock! I'm standing here on this 50-foot billboard over the Santa Monica freeway, and you think I'm upset. Of course I'm upset."

"Don't get so upset, kid. Whassa problem?"

"Why should I tell you? And who are you anyway?"

" I work here, kid. I'm a billboard artiste."

"What did you say? Billboard teacher?"

"Artiste! Agent provacateur of the advertising world!"

"All right, don't get so upset. What are you, um, painting now?"

"Cindy Crawford. Look close, right on the mole above her lip."

"Wow! Does it really say that?"

"Dunno, kid. I want to know someday. I'll have to get it in Gere."

"Ahhh! I'll jump!"

"No, kid. Can't you take a little artiste humor? You were going to tell me your problem."

"No, I wasn't. Why should I? You won't understand, anyway. It's about oratory."

"Hey! Oratory! My favorite event! "

"Huh? You're kidding."

"No, I'm Frank. And I used to be a top flight competitor in the sacred halls of oratory. I had one of my oratories reprinted once."

"Wow, in a textbook?"

"No, in a videotape. It was on subliminal advertising, and they just flashed it for a fraction of a second. Hey, wait!"

"I told you. Anymore bad jokes and I'd jump!"

"Look. Whassa problem with your oratory? Poor delivery? Too many ums and uhs? Stage fright? You run out of Depends at a tourney? What?"

"No. I can't even get to a tournament. I can't get a decent idea."

"What! How about subliminal advertising?"

"Nix on that! You have to offer a solution. Then you get some judge who just got out of an impact debate round, and he lists six d/a's on the ballot and gives you the eight."

"Hmm. How about a warm fuzzy? Like 'don't be afraid to be yourself'?"

"No wonder you've got this job. Those went out with the selfish eighties. They'll beat out the problem — solution oratories, but they're just fluff. Get in the final round and everyone makes fun of it. I saw a final round when a girl gave a speech on 'reach out and touch someone' and five guys got sued for harassment."

"So what's left, kid?"

"How should I know? My coach says that a winning oratory has to provoke thought. Thought! I haven't had one of those in months!"

"Go ahead. Jump!"

"What?"

"First you barge in on my studio. Then you insult my sense of humor. You put down my vocation. And now you refuse to think! Jump!"

"I thought. . . ."

"Ah! You can! Just on a primeval level! Kid, there are millions of thought provoking subjects. Just open your mind and feel."

"Where! WHERE!"

"Here look at this."

"*Harper's*! My grandmother reads this!"

"Maybe that's why she lived longer than you will. There are, oh, maybe two hundred fabulous oratory subjects in this magazine, dated December 1994. LOOK AT IT!"

"Don't be pushy! Um, strike that. But where do I look?"

"Take a highlighter - here, use my purple one. Now, highlight every topic sentence you see. Assuming you know one when you see one. Here, let me do one for you."

In the Temple of Pain by Paul West
Harper's, December 1994, p.29-30.

1. To (the doctor) I was just an item in a long chain of cases, rather like an author to a literature student, reading a survey volume.

2. What both groups (of doctors, good and bad) had in common was almost a total ignorance of the fact that a sick patient was not someone to spar and argue with. (preposition in the original)

3. Doctors should realize that patients — those who suffer — come from a different dimension, where in vainglorious optimism, they hope to prosper without medical aid.

4. Why do doctors think pain is good for people?

(5. The trouble with medicine is that it sees itself as a religion.)

"OK, kid. See any oratory there?"

"Good heavens. They all could be oratory subjects! Either five or one!"

"Yep. Now you do one. I'll make it easy — do the cover article."

Life as We Know It by Michael Berube
Harper's, December 1994, p.41-51

1. Looking over the fossil record, I really don't see any compelling logic behind human's existence on the planet.

2. But what's odd about Down's is how extraordinarily subtle it can be.

3. There has never been a better time than now to be born with Down's Syndrome.

4. There really is a difference between calling someone a "mongoloid idiot" and calling him or her "a person with Down's Syndrome."

5. It's impossible to say how deeply we're indebted to those parents, children, teachers, and medical personnel who insisted on treating people with Down's as if they could learn, as if they could lead "meaningful" lives.

(6. And yet there is something very seductive about the notion that Down,s Syndrome wouldn't have been so prevalent in humans for so long without good reason.)

"I see only one, admittedly incredible, subject."

"You're right. You don't think. Look again."

"Ahhh. I see an oratory on human differences. I see a defense of political correctness. And there is a speech on the value of human life."

74 A Tool For Forensics — Individual Events

"Good job, kid. I thought you could do it. And at that next tournament, when you're up there on that platform in that final round, say hi to Mr. Lincoln and Mr. Douglas for me."

"AHHH
    HHHHH
        HHHHH
            HHHHHH"

I Can See You Naked

(originally published 1995)

The crowd hushes. The orator, last speaker in the final round, moves toward the front of the room. He looks at the judges, who nod their heads. He glances down, then looks every member of the audience directly in the eyes. He says

"I Can See You Naked."

It's the title of a book. Your stampede to purchase it might be slowed by passing on the subtitle *A Fearless Guide to Making Great Presentations*. The author is Ron Hoff and he has some of the greatest tips an orator could ever use — not to mention everyone else in the communications field.

The ideas I'm going to explain to you come directly from the book, but with a few of my own examples. The subject is what that mythical speaker above either had or did not have. And the instant he stood up to speak, you knew it.

Presence.

I've tried to explain presence to my classes, but the best definition came from a freshman. Presence is when you are THERE. Really there. Ronald Reagan has presence. George Bush does not. Robert E. Lee had presence. Ulysses S. Grant did not. Bart has it. Homer doesn't.

When you consider that judges make up their minds about whether you are in the top or bottom half of the round within the first thirty seconds of your presentation, this element of presence is critical. And it is not something that only a precious few have been blessed to enjoy. Anybody can capture the quality of presence. Some of us have it naturally, others of us must learn it.

So let's analyze it.
What are the elements of presence?

1. **Openness.** The presenter moves with a purpose that envelopes the entire room. The attitude is outward, not inward, concerned with their own problems. Take two musical performers. One takes the microphone gingerly, the other seems to pick it up as an afterthought, just before the cue. Meanwhile, the open performer looks at the audience. A smile crosses her lips. The audience leans forward, expecting a great performance. This means a feeling of

2. **Positive anticipation.** We can hardly wait for the presenter to speak, because they are eager to perform. There is nothing about them that suggests reluctance. They want that spotlight. They seem to reach for it because

3. **Nothing is tentative.** They are prepared and here they come!

4. **They move.** Now, you probably cannot walk during an oratory into the audience a la Donahue, but you can use the front of the room and especially you may use the attitude of your body. How much of your time do you spend standing straight up, with your shoulders still and the center of your body in your chest? That is static and eventually boring to your audience. MOVE! Lean to one side, bend at the waist, turn to the side. Gestures can actually cross the body, you know. We are not limited to the Classic Debater Chop. And speaking of chopping,

5. **They look good.** This is seemingly bad news to those of us who are aesthetically challenged. But looking good does not mean looking beautiful. It means for the gentlemen:

The clothes fit. They are pressed. The tie is tied correctly, the shoes are clean, the socks aren't left over from gym class, and the hair is not in the eyes. For the ladies:

The clothes fit. They are not causing you to bust out all over, if you catch my drift. The shoes are not causing you to wobble like a new born colt. Makeup is minimal, and most importantly, the hair does not obscure your most important element of your presence — your eyes. For all:

You look healthy. You look at the judge(s) and a miracle occurs.

You smile.

I cannot recommend anything that will instantly add to your success more than a genuine smile that establishes a spark of communication between you and the judge(s). Of course, in adversarial American education, this is somehow considered a ploy — kissing up. How very sad. Our opinions of people who smile are not merely influenced in the way that we like them — we feel comfortable with them, too. In smiling at a judge, you are defusing an awkward situation not only for you, but for the critic.

6. **They expect you to enjoy yourself.** This, ultimately, is the secret of all great performances, no matter what the event. Take this motto and post it in a prominent place, and recite it after attendance every day.

The performance is for the benefit of the judge.

Good things happen to people with presence. There is no reason why you should not experience these good things. Presence is for all year, not just birthdays and Christmas.

Sorry.

How Interp Could Learn From Baseball

(Originally published 1995)

So, you're a tad inconsistent.

Some rounds you're ready for the Academy Awards. You nail those characters: the hero is lovable, the villain despicable, and you leave the judge marveling at your talent.

And then — hoo boy! The next round you are as flat as the ocean in the doldrums, and not even as exciting. The highlight of your performance, AND THE JUDGE YAWNS.

Well, that's drama, right? That's the old comedy circuit, si? Some nights Robin Williams can't get a laugh, and even Laurence Olivier filmed *The Boys From Brazil* (trust me, don't see it).

It's all luck. Or hormones. Or something.

Well, you're right. With the way you are approaching your piece, it IS luck. But it doesn't have to be as random as all that.

Let me start to put this in perspective. Let's say I offered you cold, hard moolah for every top rank you pulled down. In every tournament this year, I'd offer you five hundred smackers for every one, and since I'm a great guy, one hundred for every deuce.

How would that change your approach to a tournament?

Let's be honest, it would transform you, right? You would be much more focused, and much more prepared. And the rankings would soar.

Well, maybe.

The problem still is the lack of consistency. Your best performances, when everything goes right, are the product of a blending of controlled energy and adrenaline — you're pumped, but still under control. But that happy recipe isn't easy to duplicate, as you prove the very next round.

Our cousins over in athletics have a lot to teach us. They, also, are looking for that secret blend of performance ingredients — control with energy. And since they have major incentives — a stadium full of critics, college scholarships, and screaming members of the opposite sex — they have discovered ways to more consistently mix the recipe. And there is no reason why we cannot borrow what they have discovered.

The secrets are called focus, checkpoints, and energy.

FOCUS — Mike Hargrove, now the manager of the Cleveland Indians, was a pretty fair country hitter in his day. Though he wasn't a home run threat, line drives leaped off his bat with, you guessed it, consistency. He was also absolutely infuriating to watch.

Before every pitch, Hargrove went into a routine: unstrap the batting gloves, strap them on again, tug on the cap, pull on the shirt, one foot in the batter's box, tap the plate, other foot in the batter's box, short swing, touch the gloves, waggle the bat — are you ready yet, Mike??!! He was known as the "Human Rain Delay."

The routine was his way of focusing on the next pitch. Let's follow him through it. Unstrap the gloves (*the last swing is over, forget it*) strap the gloves (*use the wrists*) tug on the cap (*think!*), pull on the shirt (*use the body*), one foot in (*what if the pitch is outside?*), tap the plate (*where is outside? Don't swing at it!*) other foot in the box (*quick feet!*), short swing (*where is inside?*) touch the gloves (*how far away is inside?*), and finally waggle the bat (*quick hands, quick hands!*). Hargrove was ready to bat. Everyone else was ready to go to sleep, but hey, Mike was ready!

In contrast, have you watched the scene in *Bull Durham* where Crash Davis (no relation, my performances go Thud) is fooled by the pitcher and strikes out? Notice how he thinks differently on every pitch, and he thinks himself right out of the picture. Does that look familiar to you?

Just review Hargrove's routine, and you can see a complete checklist for a performer in dramatic interp or humorous interp! Let me give you the checklist of one of the best performers I have ever seen.

- ✔ Wash your hands (last round is over)

- ✔ Dry your hands slowly (use them!)

- ✔ Shrug, bounce on the toes (where's the center of my body? Use it!)

- ✔ Deep breath (character # 1's voice)

- ✔ Dip shoulder (here's the center of gravity)

- ✔ Wipe the face (here is the master gesture)

- ✔ Speak a line (here the character is! Ready? If not, go over the entire routine again.)

- ✔ Same for character #2

- ✔ Same for character #3 etc.

- ✔ Are all characters ready? Where am I tense? Shake left leg. Shake right leg. Shake hands. Twist neck. Dip head.

- ✔ (Ready to enter the room) Where are the judges? Who talks to whom? Step back, breath one, breath two, breath three, step forward, **GO!**

This routine could take my actor as long as thirty minutes. He was very disciplined, and maybe you're not. But what do you have better to do in that thirty minutes?

CHECKPOINTS — Now let's tackle the second ingredient in the great performance recipe. For this lesson we turn to golf and bowling.

Lee Trevino has won a few tournaments in his career, which has been a long one. At times, he has been fabulously hot, winning or placing in almost every tournament. Other times, he can't win a bet on how bad he will be. And the source of his glory or his shame has always been his putter.

Trevino tried everything — new stances, new putters, prayer — nothing worked consistently. Then, in an attempt to get his mind off his troubles, a buddy took him bowling, and Trevino learned about "spots."

You've seen them on the lane. You focus not on the pin, but on the spot. It's closer, and you can hit the spot more consistently than the pins. Trevino, watching his buddy clean up by spot bowling, decided to try it with his balky putter.

Yeah, it worked. But for our interest, Trevino added a twist performers can borrow. As he played a round, he would note how well he was hitting the spots. (How well he was sinking the putts was a question of reading greens, more than his stroke). After practice, he soon knew where in his stroke he must be pulling or pushing, because that was the ONLY WAY HE COULD MISS THE SPOT.

The lesson — as you practice, there are certain high points in your piece that give you the opportunity for checkpoints. These are emotional moments that combine an effect with a pause. Use the pause to accomplish three points on the list

        A. Did I hit the pause effectively?

        B. If not, why not?

        C. OK. here's what we'll do about it.

But you say, that will make me more inconsistent. Not if you are properly focused entering the round. Recall that each character "checked in" before you began. So, which character checked out so that the scene isn't working? Hit that character hard in his next appearance, and the scene may be rescued.

Of course, you can only do this if you are under control, and that is how the last ingredient announces itself to you.

ENERGY — and for this secret we go to track.

Being from Kansas, I have the usual hero worship for the great miler, Jim Ryun. Jim used to run the back roads of our state, daily proving to his exhausted body that Kansas is not flat. He also discovered something about his "kick" — that something extra that he summoned to beat an opponent. He found that if he had done something to lose a certain store of energy earlier in the day, or even weeks earlier in his training, that the kick would be unpredictable.

Notice I didn't say that the kick wouldn't be there. Ryun was dedicated to his sport, and whenever he summoned something out of his body, it usually answered. But a too powerful kick could be as devastating as the opposite — it could throw him off stride at a critical moment.

Ryun finally discovered that the critical moment was breakfast of the day of a race — and this discovery, properly studied and published, lead to the fairly common sports practice of power eating carbohydrates at critical times in training for a performance.

This is probably going to make you unhappy with me, but here goes.

1. Eat breakfast. A good one. Yeah, you're nervous. But come ten o'clock, the nervousness will be gone, and your body will be famished.

2. Don't pound simple sugars. Snarfing the Snickers bar thirty minutes before the last prelim round will give you a surge of energy, but at a terrible cost: the surge will not be controlled, possibly putting you over the top; and it may leave you exhausted for finals, where no junk food will bring you back.

How Interp Could Learn From Baseball

3. Don't leave your energy on the bus, or hanging out with the buds. But you say: "if I don't hang out, I'll be too nervous." Consider this — entering the round, your denial mechanisms will either succeed or fail, in stopping that gut wrenching surge of adrenaline that you fear. If it fails, then you're out of control, and disaster awaits. If it succeeds, then without nervous energy, your performance will be dull and lifeless. I have found that the folks in finals are generally those who disappear from the crowds most of the day, coming to terms with their bodies and minds.

I sound like your mom, right? That's O.K. When it comes to knowing what increases or decreases quality of performance, turn to your sports heroes. You can hardly expect to do less and be consistently successful. Then even though my offer of paying you for forensics performance was hypothetical, maybe I'll end up paying you money: to see you in the movies!

Statue! Gesundheit!
or
I Lava the Great Ideas
(Originally published 1989, revised June, 1995)

The museum was cool and dark, and only the stars saw the Student entering the Gallery of Art. The gallery was also closed, so the Student was breaking along with the entering. Soon he stood before the famous statue that he had risked his reputation, grades and designer jeans to visit — the stone masterpiece of Rodin — the Thinker. As in all the pictures he had seen, there was the nude figure of a man, exquisitely formed, pondering some unexplained idea, concentration lovingly formed on his brow by the sculptor's prowess.

The Student fell to his knees. "Oh Great Symbol of Thought, I have risked my reputation, grades and designer jeans in those dusty air vents..."

And to no one's surprise, Buddy Reader, the statue spoke. (I would have said Dear Reader, but those harassment lawsuits...) "Jeans!" moaned the statue, "What I would give for a pair of Levis. The air conditioning in this place is murder! Let me borrow your jacket, huh?"

"I'm sorry. I didn't wear one."

"Why do you think I'm hunched over like this? Last stages of frostbite, that's why. So, enough of my problems, kiddo. Why the long face? You look like that self portrait of Van Gogh over there."

"I wanted you to lend me an ear..."

"Shh! Not so loud! You'll offend him."

"So sorry. My problem's simple. My coach entered me in original oratory next month at districts, and I don't have an original thought in my body."

The statue grumbled, and a fragment fell as he wrinkled his brow. "Facial expressions are murder, ya know? Think, kid. You can find a topic. You asked the usual questions?"

"Such as?"

"What subject gets you really angry. I mean, so mad you can spit?"

"Um, when they pre-empt "Happy Days" for a presidential press conference?"

"Hmmm... Well, what about the other old standby? What human quality is most important? What would make the world a better place to live in if all of us only had much more of it?"

"That's easy. Fast cars!"

"You are a hard case, kid. You sure your dad wasn't a sculptor? Sorry, sorry, that wasn't gneiss. Let me think."

"You want me to leave?"

"Just an expression. Look, kid, everyone runs short on ideas every once in a while. For most problems, people usually just sit back, relax and an idea just comes to them. The problem with stuff like speeches and marriage proposals is that the relaxation with the Walkman destroying your hearing only draws you further within yourself, and you're limited to whatever is already in your mind, and that's Frustration. What you need is stimulation from Outside Ideas."

"What's a great source for Outside Ideas?"

"Easy. I'll give you three. One of them is so obvious that I'll bet you tried it already."

"Oh, no. Not the library!"

"Natch."

A Tool For Forensics — Individual Events

"But when I go to the library, it's like the books close in. Stack after stack. It's like they're sealed in child-proof packaging."

"You're in a bind, eh? Nasty pill to swallow. Don't get angry. Thinkers have plenty of time to have pun. Look, I know the problem. Information is intimidating. All these ideas, but where to start? So, ask the librarian!"

"You ever try to ask a librarian 'I need an idea for a speech?' She looks at you like you set off the alarm or something."

"So listen. Get some books by Adler or Palmer."

"Huh?"

"Two people. Great writers, who could explain Plato to limestone (Never trust limestone. It invented the shell game). Mortimer Adler wrote a volume of the Great Books called the *Syntopicon*. It explains in plain words what the other philosophers wrote. Donald Palmer writes philosophy textbooks, except they read like essays and are illustrated with witty cartoons. I laughed so hard I lost three inches of my cheek. On my face, kid. Give me a little room, O.K.?"

"Sorry again."

"You pick up these books, and ideas just fall out of them. Lousy vandals. How they get away with it is a marble."

"Another rock joke?"

"You expected maybe Jerry Seinfeld? All right, the second place to get ideas is the lunchroom."

"You're kidding me."

"No way. All that talk is about what people think is important. It either is or it isn't. Either way is an oratory idea."

Statue! Gesundheit!

"You said three."

"You were right."

"Huh?"

"You came here. The museum and the art gallery. The very reason these places exist is the attraction of ideas. Here are the collections of Beauty. All of us here move Thinking Beings in some way. Some of us provoke awe, and others of us shame. Every Great Idea is here to be mined. You want an idea, here is your quarry."

"I think I see. But I wanted something completely different. I wanted to say something that had never been said before."

"You think that this is a collection of the commonplace? People don't talk about Great Ideas every day, that's why museums and art galleries and state ballets always struggle to keep on going. And because people do not stop to think about Great Ideas, just about any approach you take will be unique."

"So take nothing for granite, right?"

"Get out of here before I call the cops."

Lincoln-Douglas Debate

Diogenes Visits the Coaches' Lounge

(originally published 1995)

- Hey Jimbo, how did your kid do in that final round down at Ralfville South?

- Ahh, we dropped it. Didn't have a chance with that panel — two Buddhists, a Southern Baptist, and an existentialist.

- FOUR judges?

- There was a fifth guy, but he bought our 'suicide is an option' position and hung hisself with a flowsheet.

- That's nuthin, Lissen to. . .

- Hey, Winnie. Somebody out here askin' for somebody.

- So?

- Guy with a lamp. Says he's lookin' for an honest man.

- Well, show him in. How you doin' old feller? Wanna judge a round?

- Pardon me, my name is Diogenes. Are you an honest man?

- Well, I'm a Lincoln and Douglas debate coach.

- Oh, wrong room. Never mind. Do you mind if I eat some of this food on this table?

- Why not? Ain't ours anyway. Just stay out of that bean dip. It's Ralph's and he gets awful cross if. . .

- Wait a minute, old timer. Prince Di o- somethun. What's wrong with being a Lincoln and Douglas debate coach?

- There's nothing wrong. It just often isn't ethical.

- What?

- What's ethanol got to do with Lincoln and Douglas debate, Biojeans?

- Ethical. You want a dictionary definition?

- A dictionary? Well, I dunno. What are your standards for. . .

- Here it is. Ethical. "In accordance with the accepted principles of right and wrong that govern the conduct of a profession." Is L–D debate coaching a profession?

- Not if you're supposed to make a livin' at it! Yuk, yuk.

- Right. Avoid the bean dip, I get it . These Oreos aren't too stale. . .

- No, old man. We ain't lettin' you off so easy. Just what are you sayin'?

- Hmm. Lincoln-Douglas debate, right?

- Um, yeah.

- Based on values, right? Heirarchies? Make hard choices at a single bound?

- That's the theory.

- O.K. Say you are debating a tight round. The other debater makes an excellent point about the nature of humanity as bestial. Don't smirk, it's not dirty. Tell me, is it ethical for you to write a quote on the spot from a famous philosopher to negate the point?

- 'Course not. It's against the rules.

94 A Tool For Forensics — Lincoln-Douglas Debate

- Really? Show me the rule in the manual that says you can't make up a quote whole cloth. Poof! Instant quote!

- Well, even if there isn't one, we all know you shouldn't do it.

- 'Shouldn't'. A very good word. Now, your debater goes into a round where she personally knows one of the judges. Should she protest him?

- 'Pends whether he likes her or not.

- Right. I didn't have any of the bean dip. May I take a mint?

- There's no rule against havin' someone you know judge you!

- Just so. You can't make such a rule. The rule would be undefinable, besides being unenforceable. But there is an ethical standard against it. Your debater has an edge in the round, which is from no fault of her opponent. Your debater should decline the edge.

- Over my dead body she does. All that is part of the game.

- Then there should be a rule to cover it to stop this abuse. But there isn't. So what do you do?

- You do what you need to do to win the round.

- Oh? Right. Well, been nice seeing you. Could I take a handful of Doritos?

- No! I mean, I could care less about the chips, but I do resemble the remark about bein' unethical. What do you suggest? What is ethical?

- It's a very simple principle, really. *No competitor should ever reduce the autonomy of either the opponent or the judge.*

- Auto – what?

- I think that's illegal in Kansas.

Diogenes Visits the Coaches' Lounge

- Oh, sure, it is a vague concept. But the ethical approach demands that you broaden the definition as far as possible. Autonomy means the power of a person to control his or hers own destiny. It is within my autonomy to make statements about the debate, or to judge it in any way I deem fair. It is not ethical for me to take away any other person's ability to do the same. It is not ethical to deceive a judge in any way. It is not ethical to refuse that evidence be examined by either the judge or the opponent, if there is no rule against it. It is not ethical to force an opponent to use her cross-ex time to determine what the qualifications are of a quoted source. It is not ethical to drop an opponent's argument in the final rebuttal without at least saying why it is unimportant.

- Hold it! This time you've gone too far! Why is that?

- Because you have stopped being a debater and have become solely an advocate for a cause. You have taken advantage of your power as the final speaker. But instead of reducing the autonomy of your opponent, in this case you are reducing the autonomy of the judge. No longer does the judge have the freedom to compare arguments without treading on one debater's autonomy or the other's.

- I still don't get it.

- All right. (Could you open that bag of Potato Skins?) My negative opponent has presented an argument of considerable weight. In my last rebuttal I ignore his argument and continue to profess my own. This tactic forces the judge to weigh my opponent's argument against my own without my input. That is the same as lying to a person about the defects of a used car. Do we agree that would be unethical?

- Well actually, I have a fine little beauty that I would like you to look at. Only 1000 miles and driven only by a Latin teacher on the Ides of March.

- Shut up, Winnie. Face it, Doggy Knees. You want to place an impossible burden on L–D debaters.

- Impossible, did you say? Impossible to conceive that someone would refuse to take advantage of a helpless victim? Refuse to sacrifice values on the altar of value debate? Ah well, perhaps I am being naive. It is particularly poignant, however, that the activity you created to help restore confidence in competitive speech is widely recognized as being the second worst example of dog eat dog. I wonder what Mr. Lincoln and Mr. Douglas would say if they could see their names bandied about thus. Good day, gentlemen, using the term generically, of course.

- Man, am I glad he's not judgin' my kids! Next thing ya know, he'll start claimin' that all the events have some sort of ethics!

- Yeah. I wonder what the worst example is? Oh, hi, Ralph.

- Whatcha know, boys? Hey, who took all my bean dip?

Keeping Your Cool
(originally published 1994)

And today, boys, girls, and other persons, we have Mr. Canine! Say Hi, kids.

"What an interesting collection of crash dummies!"

Oho! Mr. Canine. That was truly uncalled for! How do you get up the gall to say something truly gratuitous?

"Its my job, Moose breath."

But tell us, why are you here today?

"I came to offer a few tips to those debate creeps of yours."

Those sweet children?

"Yeah. Crisco wouldn't melt in their mouths. I judged a couple rounds at that circus in Fargo? Man, I missed my calling. I coulda been a contenda. Here are four of the fanciest dressed people you ever seen. Models of the Dan Quayle school of family values."

Yes. We are very proud of these fine young people.

"But like between every speech, they have this three minute episode where everyone gets up and DROPS THE MASK OF CIVILIZATION. I mean back to the caves. Take your paws off my dinosaur drumstick behavior."

I'm sure you made a mistake.

"Don't call me what your parents called you. Give you an example. Tiny dorm room. I'm sitting on the mattresses, trying to keep up with this woman babbling her first affirmative."

Gives new meaning to the phrase 'bed spread'?

"Hey, who's the professional here? So this guy gets up, and the first question he asks is 'What was your first stupid argument?' And she turns this bright, beet red, and she spouts 'They weren't stupid.' And the guy says 'They were stupid,' and she repeats 'They weren't stupid.' The other two judges, they laugh at her. And that makes her even madder, and it was down hill from there."

But, that's awful! What did you think? Were you offended?

"You bet. Terrible, not even worth repeating. Sheer torture for a professional. Nasty sneers. Little flecks of spit on the bottom lip. Juvenile technique. I've had more fun in coaches' lounges."

And it was this way every round?

"Oh, sure. Nobody came right out and called anyone an idiot, but NOBODY ever was nice to anyone else."

So, what should we do about it?

"Well, you got two choices. One is to start bashing people who get nasty, but with the reaction I saw from the other two bozos there are some Wayne's World clowns who think diplomacy was a dinosaur. Two is to learn some basic techniques to deflect the venom."

And, as Mr. Canine, you have some suggestions.

"Of course. I can tell you exactly what I hate when I'm trying to rile somebody.

"Let's say I ask you the same question that the Neanderthal asked her. Do this. I'll even outline it so you can understand it. Title it:

WHAT TO DO WHEN SOMEONE CALLS YOU STUPID OR ANOTHER EUPHEMISM FOR SAME.

A. Pause. Nothing in the rules say you have to fire right back. Yeah, you probably can't count to ten. But I'll give you a psychological parameter. Count to three by one thousands. After you get insulted, give yourself that time before you answer. The best part is the sarcasm dangles in the air, and it gets less and less funny with each second.

B. Never repeat the insult. The girl who repeated 'stupid' just drove the insult into the judge's minds. Yeah, they were jerks to laugh at her, but they didn't laugh until she made the insult legitimate by repeating it!

C. Answer positively. This may sound impossible, particularly when you want to bite the other guys neck, but it can be done. What she should have said was 'I gave you an excellent observation, a workable plan, and a great advantage. To which do you refer?'

Now think about it. If he says the word 'stupid' again, like 'they're all stupid' he has lost all shock value and the tables are finally turned.

D. Use the opportunity of the insult to quote your solvency evidence. She should have said 'St. Vincent's thought the plan worked just fine.'

E. Here is a revenge device. When someone really zings you, it usually means they are out of control. They are the type of debater who is seized by adrenaline, and the old 'fight or flee' response dictates to them that you are the enemy. That's why they are so nasty. They are afraid of you.

"Therefore, reach out and touch them. Just the fingers on the lower part of the arm. If they are the type that likes to hide behind their boxes at their desk, walk over and lean on their table. The response will be amazing."

What will they do?

"Try it, and you'll see. Some react by nearly dislocating their shoulder jerking away from you. Others quickly settle down and become human beings again. Watch the reactions of your judge. Most judges react to the touch technique very positively, and that usually brings the creep back to reality. I guarantee, one way or another, the situation will immediately come to a head, and the nature of the cross-ex will improve. I mean, after you touch them, what can they do. Deck you?"

Keeping Your Cool

I've seen some debaters who might.

"Aha. You DO know what I am talking about. It's debate's worst little secret — the worst instinct is calling the tune during rounds, and the coaches are doing very little to stop it. You can, you know. Just listen outside of a room to one of your debaters in cross-ex, and ask yourself if you are proud of his/her/its behavior. And if you think that is what is necessary to win, read my answer in Matthew 12: 34-37."

I just did. Is it really that bad?

"Your purpose is educational, right? If such techniques are successful, what are you teaching? Next season, first weekend, if every coach immediately forfeited the first round of the season when the kids got nasty, the problem would be over."

But, Mr. Canine. What would happen to you?

"I've got new frontiers. I'm really doing well over there in Humorous Interp. Pasta la Mista, baybee."

The Last Words of Socrates

(originally published November 1987, revised June 1995)

Socrates fell back on his pallet, the last drops of hemlock dripping from his lips. With a feeble gesture, he motioned for his disciples to come to him and await the arrival of the Great Questioner. One student, Elucidates by name, was openly weeping. "Why," he moaned, "Why, Teacher, why?"

Socrates extended an aged, shaking hand to his student. Elucidates took it tenderly in his own. Then, with sudden strength, Socrates seized his students pinkie and twisted it savagely. Elucidates cried out in great pain. "Why?" snarled Socrates, "What a stupid question! All these ideas I have taught you. They even give my teaching method the name Socratic Dialogue. And here I lie, breathing my last, and some Spartanhead gibbles 'why?'"

"But teacher," moaned Elucidates" I only wished to know why you swallowed the poison."

"Ah!" brightened the philosopher, "A much better question. If only Lincolnus–Douglasi debaters could do so well! Can you be even more specific?" The disciples looked at one another. One gazed longingly at the hour glass. Another, Unctuous by name, shook Socrates quite roughly by the shoulder.

"Cut da manure, Sew-crates," (Unctuous was a Philistine), "I didn't walk thwenty miles to hear some lecthure on Gweek. . . ." But Socrates cut him short.

"Ah, you use the correct word. How would you like to sit there listening to a couple of high school geeks ask useless questions during cross-ex periods?"

Unctuous snarled "What doth miles have to do with cwoss-ex?" The students muttered to one another. "A great mind is gone," exclaimed another to no one in particular. Unctuous, thinking the comment was about him, slew the sayer, thus "slewthsayer" (because Unctuous did everything with a lisp), creating the character who appears again in *Julius Caesar*. Socrates ignored them all.

"Come here, Domino," he said to a young business type. "When I ask you a question, what do I wish in return?"

The young man looked at the others, who pointedly turned away. "Uh – an answer?"

"Excellent! Bright boy. Probably have his own business some day. Remember, home delivery is the key. But in order to answer my question, what must you know first?"

"I know! Greek!"

"I take it back. You might be a delivery boy if you're lucky. No, pupil mine, you must understand the question. What if I asked what a sky hook was. You would be unable to answer, right?"

"I got a couple of those in stock, Boss."

"Shut up, Ace. If we educated people, with so much education that it's killing us by degrees, cannot answer questions intelligently, how can we expect a high school student to do better?"

This brought several comments. "So?" "What's a high school?" "It's not killing you near fast enough if you ask me." One student shook the hour glass to see if it would go faster. One whispered to a friend "Everytime he goes on one of these tangents, time seems to slow down."

"Exactly!" cried the sage. "Because no one has figured out how to ask questions in value debate! In policy debate (and here the hemlock must have reached his guts, because Socrates screamed in pain) the listeners merely look for the subpoints and check their flowsheets. Some skip cross-ex and go worship at the Temple of Raleighus until the cross-ex is over. But in a value debate, the questioner doesn't have those signposts, or shouldn't if he is doing it right. So he must have enough background in his question to make it clear."

"But teacher," cried out Zorro (who as you remember made his Mark in the combined fields of fencing and religion, thus Zorroastricism) "We know that you value debate."

"And a heck of a lot more than those L–Drs," breathed Socrates, "Here, Z-man, take a message to Garcia. You ask questions for three reasons- clarification, to set up argumentation, or to expose the ignorance of your opponent. Of course, in policy debate — ow! that smarts! — you ask questions to avoid using prep time, but that's O.K. because everyone says c-x isn't binding, unlike my bowels, which are, at the present moment." He paused for laughter. There was silence. "Now, anyone, what does clarification mean?"

"To shed light" said G-Eus.

"And what does a light do?"

"It shows us the way. It exposes corruption. It destroys confusion!" exulted Floorlampus.

"So what's wrong with asking questions if you're confused? Is someone going to dock you quality points because you are using cross-ex for what it was intended? Now, how do you set up an argument in cross-ex?"

"Ya grab the dude by his neck and make him..."

"No, Stallonius. You must allow him to say the words that set up the argument himself. Lookie, every argument in a debate is presented for a reason, we hope. That argument is intended to lead somewhere, hopefully for the one who presents it, in a positive way. But implications always have two directions- where one should go, and where one should not."

"You mean to the left or the Right?" exclaimed Newtius.

"No, if I say that you should take some consciousness raising courses, that also means there are many things that you cannot do, if you take my advice. If you decide to take the courses, you cannot at the same time use the money you spend for tuition to help the poor, but that's not a dilemma for you, is it, buddy? Now, why do you ask questions that you know the opponent cannot answer?"

"Stupid is as stupid does."

"How did that guy get in here? You can do anything with special effects these days. No, not quite. Look, if someone quotes me, or Zeus forbid it, quotes Plato..."

"Hey, Teach! Whaddaya mean..."

"Ask them why did I write it in the first place? I can tell you, it wasn't for the royalties. That question ought to fix their chariot. Lookit, let me sum it up quickly. The Big Dude in the Sky is hoisting the stop card. Each question needs adequate background, clear relevance, and a clear purpose; those being clarification, set up argumentation, and exposure of ignorance. If we can't figure how to do cross-ex correctly, we might as well go back to policy...oops! — big mistake!" And Socrates, writhing, groaned and uttered his last words;

"Beam me up, Scotty!"

Have Gun, Will Gavel

(Originally published December 1990, revised July 1995)

WELL, SON, I GUESS YOU KNOW WHO I AM, HUH?

Uh, naw, 'cept for that tin star on yer shirt.

I'M SHERIFF PUREBLOOD, SON. I'M THE LAWMAN WHO BROUGHT IN BLACK BART, GREEN GARY AND RED ROVER. AND NOW I'VE GOT YOU, MAUVE MAX!

Looky, sheriff. Let's talk about this.

THERE AIN'T NUTTIN TO YAP ABOUT. YOU'VE VIOLATED THIRTY LAWS, TWO HUNDRED ORDINANCES AND NINE OF THE TEN COMMANDMENTS.

Aw, shucks, which one did I miss?

THE FOURTH. HOW ARE YOUR MAMMY AND PAPPY ANYWAY?

Those old coots?

THAT'S TEN.

Now, sheriff, I'm sure that this problem has somethin' to do with our li'l disagreement up at the schoolhouse.

THAT LINCOLN–DOUGLAS DEBATE? YOU BETCHA. YOU WERE ON THE SHORT END OF A TWO AND ONE DECISION, MAX! THAT'S CALLED SQUIRRELIN', AND IT'S ILLEGAL IN FOURTEEN STATES AND THE BRONX. I'M GONNA SEE YOU SWING.

But, let me explain my decision!

YOU HAD THE BALLOT FOR THAT.

But I'm illiterate.

I DON'T GIVE A HOOT WHAT COUNTRY YOU'RE FROM.

Naw, sheriff, it means I can't read nor write!

THAT NEVER STOPPED ANYONE FROM JUDGIN' AROUND THESE PARTS, YOU HAVE TO BE THE LOWEST OF THE LOW, MAX. YOU VOTED AGAINST THAT PURTY LITTLE GAL WHO WAS UPHOLDIN' FREEDOM AND LIBERTY.

But, gol darn, she never proved that freedom and liberty are valuable values.

VALUABLE VALUES! WHAT KIND OF COMMUNISTIC DOUBLETALK—

Easy guy. Why should I vote for somethin' just 'cause it's mentioned in the Declaration of Independence?

THERE YOU GO AGAIN. INSULTIN' THE DECLARATION OF UH...WHATEVER IS A VIOLATION OF TITLE SIX, SECTION A, PENALTY TO BE FOUR YEARS IN THE TAB ROOM AT NATSHUNALS.

Just listen, fer lan' sakes. Were you born respectin' your Mama and Papa?

OF COURSE NOT! BUT AFTER MY PAPPY MADE ME SWEEP UP THE COACHES' LOUNGE A FEW TIMES, I LARNED.

Gawsh, he was a mean cuss, warn't he? But respecting your Mammy and Pappy is a value, right?

SO?

So this. Values are learned. Every one, even the one about life that everyone thinks is so clear that you can't discuss it. But there are plenty of cases on records of killers who never learned to respect life. Maybe that's why they kill.

ORNERY CUSSES LIKE YEW?

Go ahead. Git parsenal, sheriff. That only proves that yew ain't larned some values yerself. Like respect for others.

I THINK YEW JES' CALLED ME A NAME. BEFORE I USE DEADLY FORCE ON YER SCRAWNY BODY, WHAT'S YER POINT?

All values are learned. Somewhere, sometime, everything we think we know somebody taught us. Since all values are learned, then all values are debatable. That purty gal claimed some core values from the 'Merican revolution and expects us to say, "Yeehaw!" Maybe some people would be so narrow minded, but negatives don't have to be. The Declaration of Independence was written by a bunch of people who owned slaves, sheriff. So much for all men created equal. But eventually we discovered that slavery was wrong, and that liberty was for everyone, not just white guys. Right?

YEAH. WE FINALLY LEARNED THAT SLAVERY WAS WRONG.

Learned! That's the point. Even "core' values have limits, and the balance between core values have to be learned, also. You should see a whole new realm of arguments openin' before those bloodshot peepers, sheriff. The value of life is mighty nice, but even the law don't hold it as an absolute. Otherwise, why would we have first degree murder, second degree murder, and horsicular homicide?

HORSICULAR?

Never mind. How about "law and order?" What a nice soundin' phrase that doan mean nuthin' at all.

HOLD ON, MAUVE. YOU'VE GONE TOO FAR.

Have Gun, Will Gavel

Give me one shred of evidence that says we are born with respect for law and order. We do quickly learn that if someone carries a gun he thinks he's a big shot, and don't pardon the pun.

I THINK I JUST GOT INSULTED AGAIN.

Someday you'll learn, tin badge.

BUT WHAT ABOUT SOCIOLOGICAL EVIDENCE, OR PSYCHOLOGICAL EVIDENCE LIKE MASLOW'S HIERARCHY OF NEEDS? DON'T THAT PROVE THAT CORE VALUES EXIST?

Maslow isn't debatable? If you take Maslow as evidence then all values are contradictory until by some freak accident they agree. Values do not equal needs.

SO HOW CAN YOU DEBATE VALUES IF THEY EXIST ONLY WHEN BY ACCIDENT PEOPLE'S NEEDS COINCIDE?

Think about it, Pureblood. Maybe you can't. Maybe all life boils down to is the moment when two pistol's spit lead and...

SPITTIN' IS A VIOLATION OF ORDINANCE.

I'll ordinance you!

Smoky here, ain't it? Billy, come try this bean dip.

The Longest Commandment

(originally published 1987, revised June 1995)

Moses went back up onto the mountain, to see if God had any more instructions that He may have thought of over the years. The bush was gone, along with the tropical rain forests, but an NFL handbook was lying in the middle of the trail, and it was burning. Out of the handbook came discordant voices, crying "flowsheet", "no flowsheet", "persuasion" and others delivered too quickly to be understood.

Finally, the Lord said "Enough." and the voices grumbled, and maybe got a little quieter. And the Lord sounded very weary. "Moses," He groaned, "You're late."

"I'm sorry, Lord, but these power matched tournaments take forever."

"I never said those were kosher, but you were flowing kind of slow that day. Look, I want to talk to you about rebuttals."

"But, Lord, you know that we serve you without question."

"Not those rebuttals. I'm talking about the new blessing I've handed down."

"Blessing? Lincoln–Douglas debate? We all thought it was a plague."

"It wasn't supposed to be anything but a blessing. Lookit, I've been judging some of those rounds and I've figured out what's wrong. The first speeches are O.K., but when the rebuttals begin it all goes to... well, it just doesn't go anywhere.

"Moses, flow this. First, about the format. I don't know why or how you got it so garbled. There really is no need to have the affirmative go last. But–since it seems to be written into stone, let's see if we can do something about it. You still with me, Moses?"

"My pen is only smoking, Lord. Keep it up."

"All right. Let's start with the negative. That rebuttal is the pits. Since the judges seem to think that anything with a number on it belongs in policy (here the Lord rumbled fiercely) most negatives just get up and repeat themselves for six minutes. I am NOT pleased."

"Fine, Lord. What shall we do?"

"It is time to go back and borrow what is good about (rumble) policy."

"But Lord, I thought you..."

"Hold it. Don't say it. You're right, I did. But even a snake has his good side, though which side that is — anyway. Tell them I want L–D negatives to more carefully develop a negative position that can be extended in that rebuttal. Write down this parable.

"There were two rabbits who were arguing over which was better, lettuce or carrots. The lettuce lover said that he loved lettuce for it's crunchy taste. The other agreed that the crunch was important, but that since carrots were crunchier the lettuce lover fed the argument, so the lettuce lover lost lavishly. Make everyone say that three times, really fast."

Moses held up the STOP card. The Lord burned it to a crisp in his fingers.

"Let me explain," said the Lord. "What is needed in that first negative speech is more than just a conflicting value. You need your own framework that you can apply to the affirmative rebuttal."

"Hold it. Sounds like policy debate to me."

"Just because something is good debate practice does not mean that it isn't good in L–D. Let's say that the affirmative claims that justice is the supreme value. The negative is well within her rights to require the affirmative to prove how that concept has become accepted."

"HER? Lord, this is a shift from..."

"Quiet! I'm onna roll! Every value has a historical framework. Go on! Tell me what the historical framework of justice is!"

Moses trembled. "Whatever you say, Big Guy?"

"What's with the Guy stuff? Don't tell me that you say it because everyone always has said it that way?"

"I think I see your point, Lord. I wrote it down, anyway."

"Good. Remember that values don't appear out of thin air. Even I have to think about 'em. Values are always the product of experience. Write that down.

"Now let's talk affirmative. Of course, it is really unfair that the affirmative gets two rebuttals and the negative only one, and any affirmative worth her salt should win."

"Oooh - there's that word again."

"Salt? Yeah, Lot's wife and all that. Lousy debater — too stiff, ya know? But anyway, most affirmatives waste the first rebuttal — you know, the four minute one. They get up and argue against the negative constructive, and really don't develop the thesis of their first constructive at all."

"Thesis?" cried Moses, "What thesis?"

"Exactly," thundered the Almighty, "Most affirmatives haven't learned a thing from oratory, or from effective advertising for that matter: to wit, a contention must always stand by itself. A thesis is developed by the summation of contentions, all leading to the thesis. The thesis should be presented both for and after the contentions, and the historical framework of the thesis is crucial...why? You wrote it down!"

"Um, because values are always the product of experience."

The Longest Commandment

"Right. Now, you tell those affirmatives that if they explain the history of a value, that rebuttal is a piece of manna. Just answer the negative's values with that historical framework in the middle speech, and then do all that hooh-hah in the last rebuttal."

"Lord, forgive me, but how do you spell that?"

"L-Y-I-N-G. Go on. Just translate that stuff and tell them."

"But Lord, this is three legal pads of the finest granite. You'll break my aching back!"

"Take two tablets and call me in the morning."

Fundamentals of the Argumentative Events
or
Your Baby is Just an Eyeball, and What's More, It's Blind!

(published 1996)

I am right and you are wrong.

That's reasonable, isn't it?

This brings us, very quickly, to the fundamentals of the argumentative events — policy, L–D, extemp and oratory.

There is only one that applies to all these events, but it is a necessary for any other step.

Viewpoint.

You learn viewpoint, and all the rest of it is just learning how to better express that viewpoint to judges.

This simple idea, however, deserves a long explanation.

Below is an Disembodied Eyeball (sincere apologies to Emerson). I know it doesn't much look like one, but that's YOUR viewpoint.

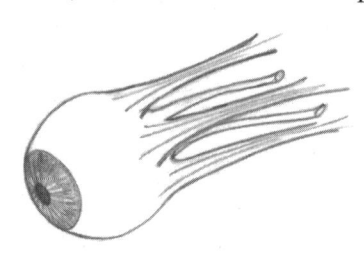

Notice that the Eyeball is seeing. This is difficult for a Disembodied Eyeball not attached to a brain, but we aren't here to be anal about it. The Eyeball sees some things, and not others. It sees the gorgeous stick figure on the street, and not the speeding car headed right at it. Perhaps the driver is distracted at seeing a lustful Eyeball.

Here is the problem. We've got reality, or The Truth if you will. But the limitations of being a simple individual in a complex world mean that we only see part of reality, and not all of it. We rely upon others to tell us what we do not know.

Those who see MORE of reality are at a great advantage over those who see less. If the Disembodied Eyeball can see both the gorgeous stick figure and the speeding car, then its chances of living to lust another day after abstract art are greatly increased.

Now, give the Disembodied Eyeball some shades. The scenery is still the same, but it LOOKS different.

Now, a well-prepared Disembodied Eyeball can see as much as it did before, but perhaps the meaning of what is seen is perhaps somewhat different. The Eyeball feels cool — Travoltaesque. It's baaaad. Therefore, the speeding car is no longer a problem. The Eyeball merely gives a "drop dead" glare and the car glides to a stop, merely nudging the plastic frames.

There is a point to this, I promise.

Now, write down the most important fact about life that you have discovered. You can make a joke of it, though perhaps it will lose some impact. Perhaps it is "Never eat at a cafe called 'Mom's'" or "Never play cards with a guy named 'Doc'". Now put these as the lenses of your Disembodied Eyeball. The Eyeball will interpret reality — the Truth — through these lenses. Therefore, the DE will not stride confidently into the cafe, expecting a good meal, or a gallery, for a sight for sore eyes. Disaster is avoided. Guys named Doc look elsewhere for their pigeons.

By now, I hope we can agree that this is a fairly accurate description of how we approach the world. It works, or it had better or we will suffer and die before our time.

Now, I approach the Disembodied Eyeball and request it's view of the world it sees. The eyeball, lacking a mouth, communicates with me (in a blink) "There is a car. There is a woman. There is a cafe." Stupid eyeball. I want to know what the Eyeball thinks about its environment. I know what I see. I even have a pretty good idea what Eyeball sees, but what I want is to know what Eyeball thinks about it.

Instead, to learn more about Truth, I want the DE to tell me about the lousy food at Mom's, and that the guy at the door named Doc is a card shark. It's what I cannot see from my own viewpoint, my own filters, that I want desperately to see.

We read fiction to see a different viewpoint from our own. Great literature affects us deeply because it gives us a different side of reality, or of Truth, than we knew before.

Have I convinced you that a viewpoint is critical in understanding the Truth? Assuming that no one in the world except Lush Rimshot has a corner on the Truth, we are most convinced of another's argument when it comes from a coherent viewpoint — that is rounded and consistent.

I'm sorry, but I've got to go back to my DE for a moment. If the Eyeball has blank spots (glaucoma?) then I am less likely to rely upon it to give a view that I can trust. I also, in judging a debate, an oration, or an extemp, recognize that the performer is wearing his shades — that even though everything that may be seen is indeed being seen, the performer is reporting only that which fits the viewpoint — the cool shades, if you will. The judge not only takes into account the shades, but is shocked when the performer has the courage to remove them. Taking off the shades and still being cool — that's STAR quality.

As you probably figured out several paragraphs before, the debater is the Disembodied Eyeball for the judge. The judge asks the Debater Eyeball to give her a view of what the debater sees. The better job the debater does in presenting that viewpoint, the more persuasive the position. The shades are the filters that the debater uses to report the "reality" of what is real — the Truth. The truly outstanding debater doesn't even seem to wear shades at all.

Fundamentals of the Argumentative Events

The same applies to all the "argumentative." events, including oratory and extemp. The judge often reacts to the blind spots of the argument — the "aw c'mon kid, don't you know this?" comment that contestants often mistake for bias. It is actually a completely legitimate protest from a person who is unwilling to be led by a person she considers "blind." Wouldn't you do the same?

Let's take an example from each genre. In policy debate, a negative looks for a viewpoint to express the negative view of the world.

Example I. Policy

Affirmative case	Negative position
	A reasonable Chinese leader MUST react violently-NOW!
I. Taiwan is oppressed by the One China Policy.	This is the solemn word of U.S. gov't.
II. Taiwan will eventually attempt to breakaway, with or without U.S. help, the result being world war! BOOM!	Any perceived favoritism of Taiwan requires a pre-emptive response, a la Pearl Harbor. If you want war, remember we will be struck first.

Plan: Recognize Taiwan now!

In the China topic, the viewpoint of the Reasonable Chinese Leader is many times the strongest, most believable view.

Solvency — the weak PRC will have to accept Taiwan's independence as a fait accompli. (OOOHH, big words!)   The weak PRC will fight a war to the death — guaranteed

Example II. Lincoln-Douglas

Aff. case on Resolved: that the rights of the accused are more important than the rights of the victim. Here I will take the viewpoint of the prosecutor.

Negative position – society is bound together with ties of confidence. Without the view that we are secure against desertion by society that we consent to be governed.

I. The presumption of innocence is the basis of justice. It is the most important right of the accused.

The conviction is the most important result of the criminal justic system. The greatest blows to confidence in government have been the failure to convict.

II. Without presumption of innocence the government will be too powerful.

The government is already bound by powerful shackles of tight budgets and limited resources.

III. Ultimately, we will all be victims in a system that ignores the presumption of innocence.

A system that is publicly foiled in protecting its law-abiding citizens cannot stand.

Implications for debaters

1. The deadliest mistake for any debater are contradictions. Look for them, and create them as decision rules. By the analogy above, no judge will be willing to follow an advocate who does not see clearly.

2. Affirmatives must establish a clear viewpoint early in the 1AC, and justify this viewpoint as superior. The opening observation should establish it, perhaps as a decision rule.

3. Rebuttals are all about viewpoints. Entire sets of arguments may be rejected simply by showing the viewpoints that create them are somehow contradictory, untrue, severely limited or unethical.

4. Any debate strategy that ultimately limits viewpoint is going to be counterproductive. The viewpoint is only as good as the consistency it expresses. Viewpoint should never be anonymous (Ehrlich in '95!). Viewpoint should never be hard to understand, else a deadly blind spot remains.

Implications for Orators
1. How about using your introduction to clearly indicate viewpoint? A common introduction is the story. The wise orator would use the same viewpoint throughout the speech.

2. Early in the speech, time must be wisely used to establish the clarity of the viewpoint, even to the extent of convincing the judge that the viewpoint is in some way clearly superior than any other. Only then can the judge relax into the flow of the speech and enjoy the argument. Speaking of viewpoint, make yourself take the viewpoint of the judge. Is doing any less showing respect to the occasion?

Implications for Extempers
1. The trend towards multiple citations can be either a boon or a blessing. When an extemper does the "two sides of this issue" approach, and then ends with a mugwump response (O.K., how about wishy-washy?) then the judge truly has not gained anything from the speech.

2. But a completely biased approach possibly offends more than the same in any other event. The extemper should not have an investment in an answer, and a too narrow answer is not appropriate. Look, Lush would not get good rankings in extemp rounds, purely because of his virulent viewpoint.

3. Bias of sources is very important in extemp. Many of the citations come from very biased sources, and some judges do realize that *Insight on the News* is published by the Moonies. This is a definite blank spot in the Eyeball. I suggest an extemper should comment on the bias of his sources, because that fact certainly affects the judge.

It may seem that I have gone a long way to make an apparently simple point, except that failure to develop viewpoint is the primary reason why you are failing to impress your judges. If that doesn't bother you, you wouldn't be reading this! Or is that just my viewpoint?

Critical Thinking and Lateral Thinking

Chapter One

As the split in the forensics community widens, it is always interesting, if you can overcome the depression, to sit quietly and listen to the judges complain.

They complain about a lot of symptoms — rudeness and speed and they say that debate, when They were around, why, that was when giants walked the earth. Meanwhile, the young coaches roll their eyes.

But the symptoms are a sign of a sickness. And the complaining about the symptoms is not going to solve the disease. Here is one person's diagnosis — the entire community, and all the events, not merely policy debate, suffer from *poor argumentation*.

Argumentation is the expression of the message — the structure and aim of the message itself. If you can accept the premise that the purpose of the community is communication, the study of the structure of the message itself should be a major component of our study. Yet I know that in my year, so many years of teaching, until recently I was pretty ignorant of the ingredients of an argument. This is scary, since I was supposed to be teaching it.

So, I went back to my own debating days (cue the rolling eyes) to the debater that I remembered best as the source of tremendous argument. And I decided, as I studied what a good argument should be, and how it applied to all the forensics events, that my idol could maybe tell me how he discovered great arguments and how to present them.

One problem — I had no idea where Geoff Goodman was, here in the late twentieth century, while I was busy searching for a good argument.

Why Iz Everyboddy Always Pickin' On Me?

            A. An inflammatory essay
                B. Why you can't answer it?
            C. Exercise - rationale
            D. Exercise I
            E. You're copping out
          F. You're still copping out
            G. Definitions
            H. Johari window
            I. Exercise II
            J. You can't catch me
          K. Why people can't stand you
            L. Homework
          M. Alternate event homework

> "He's gonna get caught. Just you wait and see.
> Why is everybody always pickin' on me?"
>   — It's a rock classic, kid. Grab some cultural literacy.

A. Being an essay on Truth in Debate

Nobody much likes us out there.

Oh, sure, we have our good reasons why we think they don't like debaters. We're smarter than the average bear, and we speak our minds, and nobody likes that much, particularly when we are right and they are wrong.

Yeah. Right. The fact is that people don't like us for the same reasons that they don't like lawyers (ouch!). They don't believe in the very premise that our passionate love is based upon — namely, that in a clash of ideas, the truth will be revealed. We consider ourselves seekers after beauty, no matter to whom she may be married at the time (George Herman, *A Company of Wayward Saints*). No one else seems to see that in us.

And the real problem is, deep in our desperate souls, we know that the principle really IS flawed. We can see in major trials that the focus is not on the truth, but on the attorneys (OJ who?). It is very clear that both sides in a trial are little interested in the truth if it gets in the way of winning.

Winning is the source of all distortion in debate, too. Look at our strategies: generic disads, squirrel cases, and critiques. Do any of these methods of winning move us any closer to the truth, except by accident? In fact, if you have ever had the pleasure of running a case with a high truth value, you probably have had the displeasure of being attacked for taking away the negative's ground.

Let's take the Ultimate Topic; Resolved: that the Status Quo should be changed. (I'll use this topic, hereafter called the UT, for my debate examples). If we ever decided to debate the UT, I'm sure every negative would lead off the 1NC with Topicality.

An example. I, the affirmative on the UT, propose that the space program should be discontinued. It is a waste of money, it creates an environment filled with falling space junk, and it removes the focus from the protection of Mankind, to the brave new world.

How can you beat my affirmative? Well, I think you might run a T argument, that the Status Quo is all we have now, and therefore to change the Status Quo you must change everything within it.

And then, you would decide to run a Patriarchy Critique, since I had the ignorance to use the exclusive word "mankind." The risk of running either argument being zero, since if you lose them it doesn't hurt you, you say, why not?

No matter that the T argument wants the judge to ignore a debate on substantive issues. And at the same time set the precedent of voting against every other affirmative case, since no case could meet the demand.

And look at the hypocrisy of the other cheap weapon, the critique. The purpose of running the critique is not Outrage, as the language critique would have you believe. If so, the last point of the critique would not be

Why Iz Evryboddy Always Pickin' On Me?

"This is a voter." Nay, it would be — "I'm so angry, I can't go on. C'mon and I'll buy you a Coke so I can settle down."

Maybe, after five minutes of procedurals to try to win the quick cheap ballot, maybe we could get to the issue at hand. I doubt it. There's gotta be generic D/A's in here someplace.

Several years ago, a student of mine attended a national workshop. A college debater literally got into his face for claiming that an argument was "the truth."

"This isn't about truth," he sprayed in his victim's eyes, "This is about debate."

No wonder we are so misunderstood.

B. That Hurt? That Make you MAD?

Gosh, I hope so. If I did my job properly, you are of two minds — do I deserve to be shot as a traitor, or will holding my head into the toilet and flushing a couple of times bring me to my senses?

I just applied the end product of this course to you, in an essay form. You may have the self confidence (some might call it conceit, but not we debaters) to think you can deny this argument easily. I remain confident that, if you are a high school debater, no matter how successful you may be, that you cannot beat my argument, BECAUSE YOU HAVE ABSOLUTELY NO TRAINING IN DOING SO. No one has EVER shown you how to attack an argument that has been prepared with the expectation that ignorant (ouch!) novice (that's a fightin' word buddy!) thinkers would attack it. It's this simple. I know something that you don't, and until you do, you don't have a prayer defeating me.

Now that's braggin' only if I can't back it up. And I'm going to let you prove it for me.

C. Exercises? What is this, math class?

Yes. Logic is math.
Friend, you can pass on the exercises if you like. But you will miss out on an incredible experience.

You ever had an A-Ha! experience? If you haven't, I mean a moment of breakthrough, where something incredibly important suddenly reveals itself in all its awesome splendor.

If you do the exercises, I promise you one. It may not leave you gasping for air like a beached fish, but it is better than sex. (All right, maybe not — just checkin' you for a pulse.)

D. Exercise the First. Right here, sucker. Right on the chin. Write down every argument you can think of to destroy the essay above. Don't cheat yourself. Think. If you're response to me is "but how do I do that?" you have had your first A-Ha!

E. More! That's a puny list, and you're not thinking a critical thought — namely what is Truth? Pilate thought it important enough of a question that he kept a mob waiting while he asked it. Look, I'm no Geoff Goodman All you are keeping waiting is an old Dinosaur with dandruff.

F. No you're not ready for me yet. Let's begin to analyze what you've missed.

G. The Parts of an Argument #1 – Definitions.

I asked you to ask for a definition of truth. If you allow me to leave that definition as nebulous as the talent of the artist formerly known as Prince, you will never be able to pin me down long enough to do any damage.

This is obvious to anyone who has ever griped about school. I daresay that includes you. Whenever you say that something is a waste of time, without defining what IS worthwhile, you employ the same slimy approach as I, except your slime is not as well-hidden as mine.

All arguments require definitions before they can be attacked. If you have ever watched a L–D round perform the "Two ships passing in the night" act, the responsibility generally rests here, on a lack of a definition.

H. So, I'll define truth. Truth is reality, encompassing not only what is perceived by humans, but all of what *is*. In fact, I am taking the same philosophical approach as the Johari Window. Have you ever seen one?

Known only by others	Known to self/ Known to others
Known by no one	Known only by self

To be brief, the window says that the truth must be larger than any one or all of us.

Understanding all of the implications of the Window is not important, though it sure is fun to argue. What is important is that I must believe that (A) The Truth exists and that (B) No human can ever know it.

I. Exercise the Second. A taste of blood? Go ahead. Make my day. Write down why my argument must fail, now that I have stupidly defined Truth in this manner. But don't cheat. You have to be good and ready before you go on.

J. I did it to you again! You can't pin me down with that definition — I'll just smile enigmatically until you give up. Lookie — if we don't know truth and can NEVER know the truth, then debate remains corrupt and contemptible. I will still win my argument, because the attackable premise is NOT anything about the Truth, but about debate and the truth.

K. Well, if you haven't torn up this paper in disgust by now, you just had an A-Ha! experience. Or I will give you one now — that the slippery technique I used on you in (J) is why people can't stand debaters. I'm playing a game with you, even to the point of including trash talk to make you play stupid. What I want to teach you is analysis — of argument, or character, or speech, and then I want to teach you lateral thinking, a technique to improve your creativity in any event. In you will carefully stick with me, we'll do just that.

L. Homework before we meet again. (For both policy debaters and L–D'rs) Think of five important conflicts that you have in your life. Number them Alpha, Omega, Epsilon, Greek, and Yo Mama. And place your attacks against the essay on the back burner; I promise you that by the end of the course, you will be just as convinced that my essay was trash as you are now. Except you will know why.

M. Homework for other events:

1. *Oratory* – take a well-written essay, and attempt to make an outline refuting it. If the essayist was the speaker in front of you in a round, what could you say to defeat his/her thesis? Or, you can do the debate exercise above

2. *Interps* – yes, this is for you. From your scripts, find three conflicts between characters. Or, you can do the debate exercise above.

3. *Extempers* – President Clinton faces choices all the time. Identify five of them. Or, you can do the debate exercise above. Do I hear an echo?

Chapter Two

What was so great about Geoff Goodman?

Well, he had plenty of success — he won the NFL national tournament, and in college he made it to the semifinals of the national debate tournament, where he gave way to another team from Southern California. But there have been plenty of successful debaters, and I fear I must say that not all of them were great thinkers.

Geoff Goodman was a thinker.

Playin' In the Sun With My Reverse Barometer

    A. Custer died for your arguments
    B. Exclusions
    C. Exclusions as cross-ex
    D. A dialogue on truth
    E. Exercise 1
    F. Good Arguments
    G. The basic map
    H. The issue
    I. Issues as questions
    J. Exercise 2
    K. Exercise 3
    L. A-Ha!
    M. The conclusion
    N. The dangers of anything loose
    O. The reasons
    P. The evidence
    Q. Evidence is not reason
    R. Evidence must be specific
    S. Braces on braces
    T. Homework
    U. Alternate homework

I will do exactly the opposite of what this man tells me to do. It's obvious what his game is. He wants to lead me away from his Indian friends. He is the perfect reverse barometer. Isn't that right, Lieutenant?

    –Gen. Custer in *Little Big Man*, right before You Know When

A. Yesterday, we began our analysis of an argument with definitions. We then apparently destroyed the value of the definitions by showing how an argument could still be effective without them. Thus, we need to encounter the second part of an argument, that serves the function of a reverse barometer to definitions. Hopefully, using this tool we will end up a bit better off than Custer.

B. The second part of an argument — Exclusions. A definition is intended to show what is going to be argued. To be effective, a definition should clearly hint that there are boundaries. What is NOT going to be discussed are the exclusions.

Take yesterday's essay. It is pretty obvious that I am speaking of policy debate, but wandering in are references that could mean that I am talking also about Lincoln-Douglas debate. Am I? Who cares?

The person arguing against the essay must, else she is again attacking a ghost. It is conceivable that I could even wiggle from talking about policy debate, since I never specifically say that policy suffers from this problem. All my examples are from policy, but never do I declare myself unequivocally. Yes, this is slimy. I'm sure you never do it. Pfui.

C. One of the miracles of cross-examination is that it allows the advocate to clearly demonstrate what the opponent is not talking about. This is not only important in policy debate, because everything that is excluded can no longer be claimed as significance or impact, but it is critical in Lincoln–Douglas because... well, you need to figure that out for yourself.

D. Let's enter into a dialogue about the essay. This is a tool that you can use to prepare yourself for advocating an argument or for attacking one. You play both roles, switching back and forth, doing the absolute best you can to represent both sides. Forget about being funny, or witty. Just be both advocates.

Idiot (I): Let's begin with this concept of truth. Tell me what truth is NOT.

Moron (M): Not Truth is lies.

I: And lies are intentional?

M: Not always. I could lie because I don't know any better.

I: Then everything is a lie. Take a look at the Johari window. Since we never can know all the truth, then there would be a lie in everything we said.

M: Oops. O.K., let me try again. Not Truth is anything that does not lead directly to truth.

I: Huh? Give me an example.

M: Simple. If I intend to show you truth to the limits of my miserable abilities to perceive and communicate it, then that is Truth.

I: Truth seeking is equivalent to truth itself.

M: In this argument, yes. Don't roll your eyes. Even if we don't know what truth is, we DO know when we are intentionally attempting to walk away from it. And debaters do this with a grin, because it is all part of the game.

E. Exercise the First. Write a dialogue about the Alpha problem you have discovered. Try to clearly define and exclude. Again, do not try to WIN the dialogue. It's with yourself, for cryin' out loud!

F. And now, argument mapping we go. When you are done with this course, immediately go buy *Good Arguments* by C.A. Missimer. Prentice-Hall is mighty proud of this book, if you catch my meaning, but it is revolutionary for us stupid people who have meditated on Toulmin and returned home spiritually ravaged. (Yes, that was a major overstatement. I learned a lot studying Toulmin. I just never could figure out how to TEACH it. The very first time I presented *Good Arguments* to my debaters, they were furious with me for never presenting it before.) Buy it and give it to your coaches — do it a nonny mouse if you think you want to — after all some coaches are as conceited as their debaters and think they know it all. I know that is hard to believe....

Playin' In the Sun With My Reverse Barometer

G. The basic concept is that an argument is like a house. I will show you what appears in the model that debaters can easily use, as a preview to what will come.

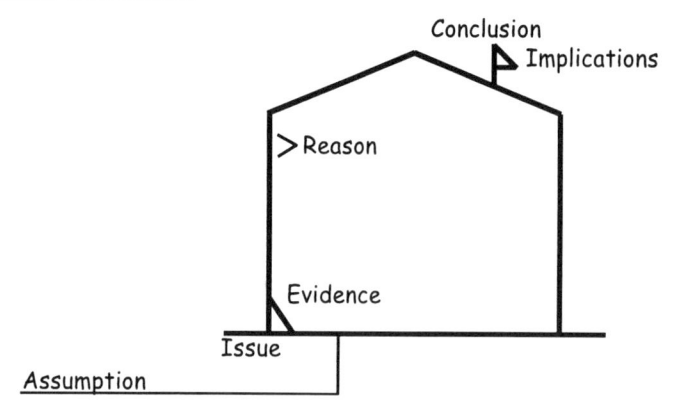

```
                    Conclusion
                        ▲ Implications
        
        ▷ Reason
        
        
         Evidence
      Issue
 Assumption
```

H. Parts of an argument – third part: The issue — the foundation of the argument. The issue is precisely what we are arguing. This can only be discovered after the process of definition and exclusion is completed: don't think that because definition and exclusion don't appear on the map that they aren't important. As a student told me, Definition and Exclusion are like real estate agents; they find where the house can be built and try to sell you the land, taking a percentage of the price, etc. etc, ad nauseum. He's a great student, but he gets carried away sometimes.

I. Issues are always expressed as questions. Statements cannot lead to conclusions — they are conclusions. Therefore, the viewpoint of the issue is a critical factor. If I inquire "What is the best pizza?", am I asking as a consumer, a businessman, or as a teacher giving a folksy example to try to impress students as being a regular guy?

> *Consumer* – Well, the best pizza is one that tastes good, is affordable, and is served in a setting that doesn't invoke Italy too much.

> *Businessman* – Money? Profit? Money?

> *Teacher* – The best pizza is Tony's Frozen Pizza, because that's all I can afford.

J. Exercise the Second. Take the consumer viewpoint, and for a moment let's grant that the criteria mentioned are valid. You realize, I hope, that if you never allow an argument to get to the building stage, that most judges will think you are the Johnny Cochrane of the debate circuit — love his taste in suits, but picky, picky, picky!

A moment's reflection should show you the difficulty of the exact wording of the issue. There are frightful consequences on either side: should you pick the Scylla of "best" as vital to your issue and then watch your opponent run amok? Or do you pick Charybdis, and get specific, paying the price of very little flexibility?

Again, my fanciful debaters returned to the model of a building for this comparison; do you build a fancy basement and spend your time constructing something many people will never see? Or do you slap your argument down on a slab of concrete, only to watch your opponent tunnel under it?

K. Exercise the Third. Carefully word the issues of each of the five problems you devised. If you don't mind making them public, then allow somebody to try to challenge them. Note your reactions as they seem to get more unreasonable than ever — don't they want to argue? Isn't that the reason for even having an issue in the first place?

L. Now you may have had an A-Ha! experience as to why people can't stand lawyers, and their cousins, namely us. The perception that we try to pick a ground that will avoid any significant discussion is justified. It is why few judges really WANT to vote on topicality, and why generic arguments are treated by so many with contempt.

M. Parts of an argument, fourth part – the conclusion. The roof of the building, and therefore all that separates a house from being a ruin, is the conclusion of the argument. Often the conclusion is as simple as yes or no, or it may be a sentence fragment, or heck, I'm feelin' generous, it could be a sentence. But if your conclusion has to be longer than a sentence, you've misunderstood what you're trying to prove, and the responsibility lies within the issue to discuss. Your teachers will tell you that the biggest fault with your reasoning powers is that they start off proving that Nixon should have gone to China, and end up convicting him for Watergate.

N. The biggest danger that awaits the conclusion is the same as that within the issue – loose wording. Go take a look again at (H) and (I).

O. The parts of an argument, fifth part – the reasons. These are the walls, that hold up the ceiling of the conclusion. It doesn't take much to recognize that the reasons are critical. The model clearly shows the danger of an assertion. Responding to your argument with "bleah" is not sufficient to justify my own.

Further it shows that one reason, no matter how well developed, is a shaky excuse for a house. In Kansas, our department of parks fell in love with concrete toadstool picnic shelters. If you go to one of our state parks, there they are. There are even ironic postcards about them "Kansas Morels." Most of us do not want funny postcards made out of our arguments.

P. The parts of an argument, sixth part – the evidence. This is the first place where Ms. Missimer proceeded to blow my mind — yes! that is exactly what evidence does — it braces up the reasons. This may not seem like an earth shaker to you, but consider...

Q. Evidence is NOT a reason. Facts, and quotes are neutral, and their existence do not create a reason for a ballot in and of themselves. Have you ever seen a debater wave a stack of evidence, and claim that is a reason to vote? Not you, right? Bah.

R. Evidence must prove the reason specifically. One or two connections are not enough. The effect of taking down a clumsy brace usually brings the wall down with it (Bob Vila, where were you when we needed you?)

S. Bracing a brace is a lousy way to build a house. A chain of evidence to prove a reason is just as weak. Consider the multiple difficulties of the generic argument. It is really a chain of arguments, and the fall of any part of any argument collapses the argument. If any quote falls, so does the chain. Pardon me, but I must say this — the only reason why generics are successful is because the debaters have accepted them, not the judges.

T. Homework – map the following arguments:

1. China poses the biggest threat of any nation to world peace. It possesses nuclear weapons, and the heartfelt belief that of all nations, it alone can survive a nuclear war. President Li Peng demonstrated this when he said to the Congress of Deputies "No one may attack the People's Republic of China, because they know they cannot defeat us."

2. Overpopulation will cause nuclear war. First, X tells us that overpop is critical to political stability. Second, Y screams that political instability is always a pretext for war. And finally Z whines that in a nuclear age, the incentive for any power that holds nuclear capabilities is to use them.

3. The US must stay out of Chinese internal affairs. History teaches us that the Chinese regard American foriegn policy as a reverse barometer — whatever they want us to do, why I shall do the opposite. Isn't that right, lieutenant??!!! Duck your head! Ouch, he got the point.

U. Homework for the other events

1. *Interpers* — Take the three conflicts from the scripts you chose yesterday. Map those conflicts.

2. *Orators* — Map the arguments from the essay you chose yesterday.

3. *L–D'rs* — Map the argument "Justice is the pre-eminent human value."

4. *Extempers* — you are President Clinton, discovering that not only does Iran have the nuclear bomb, but one is planted in the U.S. Senate. Map the argument to justify your decision.

Playin' In the Sun With My Reverse Barometer

Chapter Three

I didn't see Geoff Goodman in high school while he was winning NFL in the late 60's. Instead I was a regular victim when he was debating for USC. Thanks to Mr. Goodman, I have never had the necessity of visiting a proctologist in order to view my posterior.

He seemed tall — at least I remember him as tall, and he had a perfect "natural" — a 'fro' for white guys. It added to his height. And when he started to speak, it would bob and move as if it had a life of its own. My deaf girl friend, who watched one of Dr. Goodman's operations on my ego (while I was wishing for sixty minutes I too could be deaf), said he had "the mane of a snake charmer."

He also had a taste for theater. He liked to keep his audiences waiting — I believe that we have prep time in part as a response to Geoff Goodman.

But he could think. I never saw him run a predictable argument. For a couple of decades since, I have tried to figure out where he found those arguments. At times I wanted to just ascribe it to talent, as if certain thinking could never be taught. I never gave up the idea that I could figure out his secret, because he had to have one. I kept the flowsheets, and transcripts of some of the final round debates where he appeared, and once in a while I dug them out and studied them for The Secret. No luck.

Assume Nothing

A. The assumption
B. Examples of assumptions
C. Comparing the homework
D. Assumptions of the homework
E. Exercise 4
F. The answers - well, sorta
G. Your assumptions arguments
H. My assumptions arguments
I. Assumptions in your arguments
J. Homework
K. Alternate event homework

> "Children today are arrogant, gobble their food,
> and show no respect to their teachers."
> —Socrates

A. The parts of an argument – seven – the assumptions. Up to this point, the argument model isn't too startling. In fact, it looks a whole heck of a lot like a flow sheet; the conclusion is the advantage, the reasons the subpoints, the evidence the, um, evidence, and the issue the resolution in question form. But now we enter the dirty little secret of arguments — what it is like underneath the foundation, where the Good Arguments Are.

Assumptions are what must be true for the argument to be true. If the assumption is not true, then the argument must be faulty.

B. A couple of examples. I tell you that Pizza Hut makes the best pizza (note to self — call Pizza Hut and see if they will subsidize this blatant commercial reference). When you ask why, I tell you that PHP has the tastiest sauce. The assumption is that tasty sauce equals the best pizza.

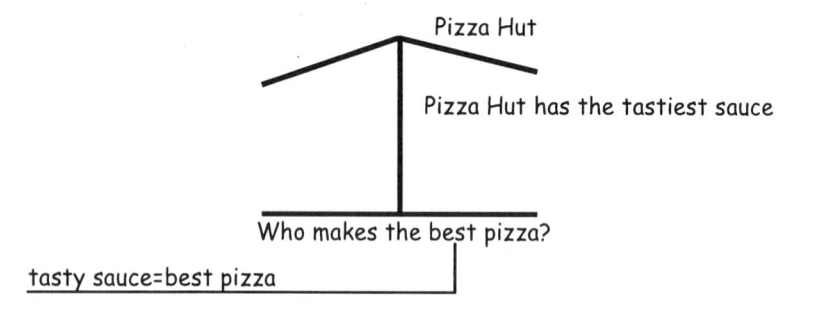

```
                    Pizza Hut
                   /\
                   Pizza Hut has the tastiest sauce

                   Who makes the best pizza?
tasty sauce=best pizza
```

Starbuck says to Lizzie in The Rainmaker: Lizzie – look at me. Look at me. When you said you were pretty, you were.

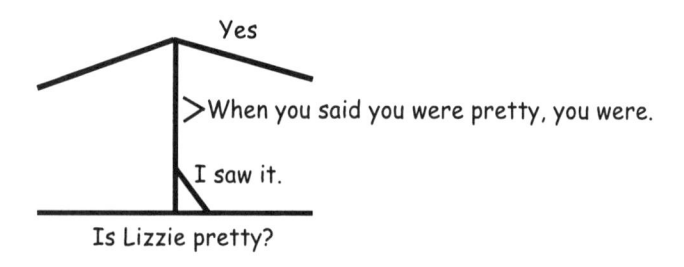

```
                    Yes
                   /\
                   > When you said you were pretty, you were.
                   \ I saw it.

                    Is Lizzie pretty?
```

140 A Tool For Forensics — Critical Thinking and Lateral Thinking

C. Take a look at the arguments that you mapped for today. Compare them with mine. The exact wording is not usually crucial (though it can be). If you and I disagree on what is the issue, or the conclusion, or the reasons, or most critically, what is evidence, then you need to take a step back and review.

D. Now, let's look at the assumptions of the argument. Some of the arguments have just one assumption, and some have many more. But all have this in common — it is an unstated warrant (as Toulmin would have loosely put it) that must be accepted before the argument can be taken seriously.

E. Exercise the First. Map the following arguments, including the assumptions. I apologize that these examples come from an Old Debate Topic, but they still work well for the UT. Take your time — you won't get anything if you skip on to my answers.

All quotes for this exercise are from Donald and Constance Shanor, *China Today*, 1995

1. The greatest risk to the Chinese Communist Party leadership in pursuing the nascent free-enterprise system it has labeled the socialist market system is the loss of its own power and control. China's leaders have wholeheartedly embraced Western technology and welcomed the foreign investment that has been crucial for industrial modernization, but the reforms and the opening to the world have led inevitably to a relaxation of the total government control that once permeated daily life in China. (p.9)

2. The most favorable course is one derided by both the conservatives and the current liberals, which is to accept the plea, the dissident Wei Jingsheng made in 1979, and paid for with fourteen years of political prison: Modernize the political system as you modernize the economy. Rule through sharing power, not dictatorship. (p.13)

Assume Nothing

3. The pragmatism and flexibility Beijing has shown in the past to further economic reforms might be stretched to encompass limited political liberalization. If the pressure from below or within the party is strong enough, the post Deng leaders may see the writing on the wall and find a face saving but satisfactory way to allow diverse voices to chart the future, using those most Chinese of desired Chinese characteristics — harmony, stability and unity. (p. 248)

4. Human rights in China touches a whole series of raw points in the Sino-American relationship, beginning, as always with history. To the Chinese, American members of Congress or human rights activists speaking on the subject bring back memories of the American missionaries preaching about salvation early in the century... China is an old and proud country, but also one that has been very weak. Any perception of interference in China's internal affairs brings out not only understandable nationalistic reactions but also fears rooted in history. (p.30)

F. Let's compare.

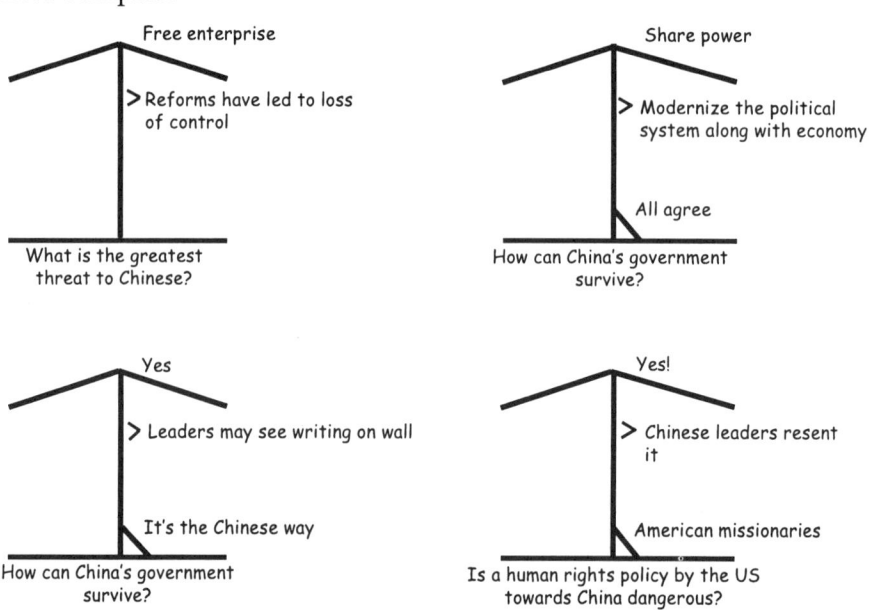

Free enterprise
> Reforms have led to loss of control

What is the greatest threat to Chinese?

Share power
> Modernize the political system along with economy

All agree

How can China's government survive?

Yes
> Leaders may see writing on wall

It's the Chinese way

How can China's government survive?

Yes!
> Chinese leaders resent it

American missionaries

Is a human rights policy by the US towards China dangerous?

G. Now let's see what the assumptions we have identified will do for us. You go first. As long as you have correctly identified the assumptions, a wide range of alternatives are available. Again, do this first, then go to what I think.

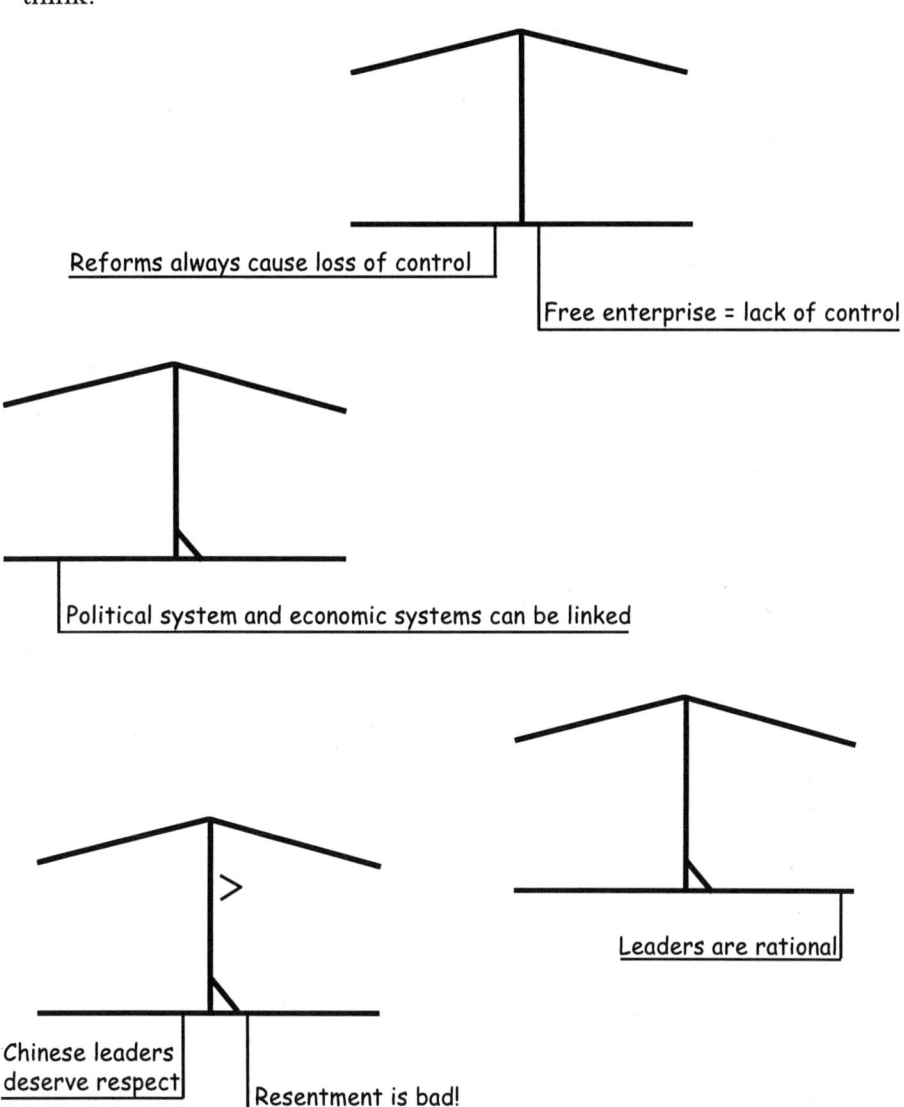

Reforms always cause loss of control

Free enterprise = lack of control

Political system and economic systems can be linked

Chinese leaders deserve respect

Resentment is bad!

Leaders are rational

H. Here are the arguments I see. Each is set up easily by cross-ex questions, which the other side had BETTER answer the way the assumptions demand they should. What should I argue if the opponent denies the assumption, or, more stupidly, refuses to answer?

Assume Nothing 143

I. Now, go back to the five arguments that you began clear back on Piece One. Map the argument, and meditate upon the assumptions, and draw them in also. Don't forget the evidence!

Alpha

Omega

Epsilon

Greek

Yo Mama

J. Now, practical application.

> Taking a possible case on the UT, the affirmative claims that the teaching of evolution should be halted in the public schools. Analyze the quotes below, and attack! (from I.L. Cohen Archeological Institute of America, *Darwin was Wrong*, 1984)
>
>> A cell has no capacity to decide by its own wit, to change its own DNA sequence and create a different alignment of 50,000,000 other nucleotides. Then and only then, would we have obtained a new species, and even then, if the sequence was not purposefully constructed, no viable species would ensue. (p.207)
>>
>> I wrote this book also because I am troubled - troubled with the rigid dogmatic position taken by a number of evolutionists. They imply that they — and they alone — know the truth. As such any further questioning is to be considered superfluous. There is little difference between the certainty expressed by such modern powers that be, and those who imprisoned Galileo and threatened him with torture for writing that the Eath was circling around the Sun. Then, too, the authorities knew exactly what the "truth" was — or so they thought. (p.6-7)
>
> Now map the argument. Here is a good example of assumptions necessary not only to the reason to be true, but assumptions necessary for the evidence to be accepted.
>
> Be ready to deliver this argument tomorrow. Make sure you include necessary cross-ex questions.

K. 1. *Orators* – what are the assumptions of the essayist you have used in the previous homework?

   2. *Interpers* – The concept of assumptions is much the same as the concept of subtext. Have you encountered that idea? It is critical, go explore it immediately. If you understand subtext, then on the maps of the conflicts from your scripts, draw in the assumptions.

3. *L–D'rs* – map this argument, loosely adapted from *How to Argue and Win Every Time* by Gerry Spence.

    God only exists because we give power to Him. If we kept all the power that we grant to God — creation, morality, control over Nature — we would not need Him.

4. *Extempers* – go back to your homework on the bomb under the Senate. What are the assumptions of your argument? Are they humane? Do they involve the use of power that the President does not have?

Chapter Four

I decide that I must find Geoff Goodman. I don't have the money to hire a private detective. But I have seen the name of the colleague of Goodman, King Schofield, still a high school coach in Souther California and a debate deity. Here is my key, but where in Southern California?

NFL should know.

NFL thinks it knows. Westlake. Phone number unknown.

Westlake High School has never heard of a King Schofield. I admit that it is a name that would stand out in any faculty. The person who answered the phone sounds somewhat harried. Perhaps it is because there is someone screaming in the background.

Back to NFL. Marilyn knows. Of course, Marilyn knows! Knows is her last name.

- Try Harvard School..

- What's the number?

- Try directory assistance.

- Yes, I know a King Schofield, but he teaches at the middle school.

- Yes, he's here. I'll transfer you.

Deep breathing exercises — I couldn't be more nervous if I was waiting for Kevin Costner to get on the line.

In Which The Author Becomes Rather Kinky

In Which The Author Becomes Rather Kinky

      A. Debating the averge house plant
      B. The implications
      C. Implications for interp
      D. Exercise 5
      E. Comparing results
      F. Implications spin-offs
      G. Use of cross-ex in implications
      H. Cross-ex in L–D
      I. Exercise 6
      J. Engulf and devour
      K. What is 'engulf'
      L. What is 'devour'
      M. Exercise 7
      N. What your mother did to you
      O. Homework
      P. Alternate event homework

> "Feed me, Seymour, feed me!"
> – a certain house plant
> (You haven't heard of this? Shame on thy head)

A. Have you debated such a house plant before? I've had a few on my debate squad. They enjoy twisting arguments, and claiming that you are somehow "feeding their argument".

Of course, most of the time, it's a lie, or a product of overheated minds — kind of the debate equivalent to "Melrose Place." However, you are now ready to truly learn what "Feed Me" really means.

B. The parts of an argument – eight – the implications

This means the end result of the argument. We don't usually bother to present arguments that have no end result — the reason why we make them in the first place is to move on to something that we think eventually will win the debate (or the desired ranking) for us. The implications — what the argument, if accepted, asks us to DO is shown by a weather vane on the top of the house. In debate terms, this is really what we mean when we jargon (jar-gone, v: to speak as an attorney, and educator, or a debater) that an argument has *impact*. More on this later.

Take this argument. I prove to you, or at least you will assume that I do, that evolution is called a theory because it is not proven. What will be your response?

It had better not be "Oh, nuttin'. Just a burp." No, there is an agenda behind this argument. The poser of the argument wants us to accept it so he/she/it can force us to grant an impact, potentially killing us all ten times over.

The implication of this argument is that if evolution is merely a theory, then there is no justification in presenting it in a public school with tax dollars without presenting, without refutation, the theory of creationism. If I have won that implication, by your default, then I have easily won the UT.

C. Every speech by a character in an interp has implications. Else, why would the speech be included in the script, anyway? The power of a scene rests in its conflict — and the implications are the expression of that conflict.

D. Exercise the Here – I'm lazy – use the ones from (3)E of Chapter Three. (You will soon see that we all are lazy.) Map the impact of each of these arguments.

E. I'll show you mine if... never mind

1. Implication(IM) – a market economy move will eventually cause a lack of control in China

2. (IM)Action must be taken to bring about modernizing of the political system.

3. (IM) Political liberalization should be a desired outcome for the Chinese.

4. (IM)Never twist the tail of a dragon.

In Which The Author Becomes Rather Kinky

Yes, there are many more implications, I just grabbed ahold of a couple.

F. Arguments that spin off implications are very profitable, because they immediately put your opponent at a disadvantage. On the one hand, she has to win the implication (impact) in order to outweigh the consequences (good old policy maker paradigm). But, if the argument really HAS impact, the implications of the argument almost never match the plan.

An example:
On the UT, the affirmative wishes to paint the walls of every public classroom a deep, relaxing green. The affirmative proves that school is very stressful, and therefore any tool possible to relieve stress tool should be used.

Now, don't go after the assumptions, though admittedly they are very weak. The implication is that we should do anything to relieve stress, therefore, I propose the ultimate solution — abolish school! Stop cheering.

G. Cross-ex plays the critical role in setting up implication arguments. The first question is to confirm that the opponent agrees that the argument indeed has that implication. The second question commits him to following the implication to the bitter end.

Take the example above.

Cross-ex
Q. So, you are arguing that school is stressful, right?
A. Extremely. I'm on 2000 cc of Maalox a day.
Q. So anything that can be done to relieve stress is a good thing?

Here is the rock and hard place. If the answer is yes, then killing bad teachers is justified. If the answer is no, then all the affirmative work is for naught — they have given no decision rule at all.

H. Of course, in Lincoln–Douglas cross is even more important, because it not only sets up a value but it also avoids the ships in the night syndrome. L–D'rs take note. You need more cross-ex practice than you do speaking practice. There are lots of good exercises in cross-examination manuals for budding young attorneys. Just ignore the advice how to cross-ex in the manuals. Most are worthless for high school competition.

I. Exercise the Now – draw up arguments based on the implications of the four arguments. Make sure you list the cross ex questions that MUST be answered correctly by the opponent for the argument to have impact.

J. Well, I think you are old enough to learn the most valuable tool of debate argument. It only took me until my forties to deserve to learn it, and I really resent you don't have to go through the pain and agony that I had to endure to learn it (are you cryin' for me yet? Is this a big enuf buildup yet?)

The tool is called **Engulf and Devour.**

I was told about this tool by one of the great masters of thinking, Chris Riffer. Prof. Riffer calls it "even if." I meditated upon it, and upon encountering (E&D) in *Good Arguments* everything fell into place.

The tool states: the initial stage in any argument is to decide whether or not simply to go ahead and grant the opponent's argument. If you do, then you have two options:

K. Engulf – to grant the opponent's argument, but to show your own outweighs it, or, to show that the limits of the opponent's argument, when compared to the limits of your own, show the argument as weak.

The simplest example is that my opponent argues on the UT that juvenile murderers should be executed in front of their school's student body. I grant that executions would scare students into a life of law abiding. But the time missed in class for the assemblies will cause them to miss so much knowledge that the United States will be weakened unto a Third World nation, leading to imperialist adventures and a nuclear war! Whew! You already call this "outweighs."

L. Devour – the opponent's argument is not only granted, but that it feeds my argument.

Example (on an old debate topic)
The opponent claims that a strong foreign policy on human rights gains the respect of the Chinese. I devour the argument by showing that the Chinese

In Which The Author Becomes Rather Kinky 151

respond to measures that they respect with fear, and when they fear opponents, the Chinese have historically gone to war with that opponent.

Sometimes, you can do both.

M. Exercise the Immediate – Take your five critical arguments that you mapped on 3(I). Draw in the implications, and then engulf and devour. If your arguments are not a secret, compare your engulfing and devouring with others.

N. Think of Engulf and Devour this way; your mother did this to you someplace in every argument you ever had with her. And the reason it was so infuriating is that it gave your argument exactly no credit at all!

O. Homework – Take a complete article on the debate topic. Identify five separate arguments within the article, map them, and then attack their assumptions, implications, and then attempt to Engulf and Devour them. Take your time, and work hard. It will be well worth the effort. If you haven't yet had the A-Ha! response, this exercise will bring it.

P. Alternate event homework

1. Extemp – You are in a cross- ex extemp final round. You are questioning a joker who has just suggested your argument on the bomb in the U.S. Senate. Devise a question to Engulf and Devour.

2. Orators – we have all encountered the judge who argues with your oratory. You are giving an oratory on the subject of the death of love in relationships. The judge scowls at your argument (whichever way it is going - you get to say). Engulf and Devour him.

3. L–D'rs – take an article on philosophy, and do the exercise above.

4. Interpers – Take one of the conflicts from the scripts — one of your favorites. In the conflict-argument phase between the two characters, intervene in the script. One of the characters attempts to engulf and devour the other. Rewrite the script from that moment on.

Chapter Five

King Schofield is on the line! I blurt

-Uh, um, I'm doing an article on thinking and Geoff Goodman.

A long silence. Not surprising. Thank goodness it's southern California, so Mr. Schofield is probably used to nuts on his phone. He talks me down.

- A process? Like a formal pattern? No, not really.

Samson has lost his hair, but he's still tugging at those columns of my imaginary temple.

- We spent a lot of time getting ready for certain cases. We talked a lot. On the information gathering topic, I generally set up the inherency position because it traded off with solvency. Geoff listened, and took it from there.

-Did you know what he was going to say?

-Exactly? Of course not. I didn't need to know.

I knew a few teams who worked on a need-to-know basis. But surely not my heroes!

-Did you ever reach a point where you could predict what he would say?

-Oh, once in a while. But not when he was really being brilliant. It wouldn't have been as much fun.

Mr. Schofield agrees to give me Mr. Goodman's phone number. I let it rest on my desk for a couple of days, getting nervous. It is time for Mohammed to go to the mountain, Dorothy to go to Oz, and for the Loser to go ask the Winner — How.

Where The Good Arguments Are

A. Back to our personality quirks
B. The brain is lazy
C. Stephen King, *The Birds* and *Listen to Me*
D. Sample Ultimate Topic affirmative
E. Exercise 9
F. Vertical thinking
G. Criteria/pre-empt
H. Forcing a position
I. Agreeing with the criteria
J. Trying to attack the criteria
K. The persistence of vertical thinking
L. Lateral thinking
M. Homework and the PMI
N. Alternate events homework

"She went over the flowsheet and around a minute and under rebuttals and through the constructives til she came to where The Good Arguments Are"
-slightly revised version of a children's classic

A. You may remember, we started out on the premise that debaters are a tad difficult to get along with, but that's YOUR problem, buddy. The study of argument reveals why debaters are such jerks. Read on if you have courage, or if your girlfriend is an interper. If you don't know, don't ask.

B. In order to understand the debater, we have to first understand thinking. And thinking, according to Edward de Bono, begins with the premise that the brain hates to think.

Yes, I know that the opposite is the common theme that teachers, parents, cops and insurance agents have been preaching to you since babehood. But the fact remains, you worked harder at thinking in babehood than you do now. Your education, beginning with the cradle and continuing into your So-called Life now, has been a process of learning comfortable patterns for your thinking to follow. It has been the rare experience that shocks you out of your automatic approach to life and into a new insightful experience.

C. As I write this, outside my kitchen window stupid cardinals have built a nest for the fourth straight year in the honeysuckle vines on our propane tank. I'm not being a nature-hater. For the fourth year, we await the disaster of the easy pickings that await some predator like snakes, cats, or my five year old. The honeysuckle vines are only three feet off the ground! Not a single cardinal has ever survived that fatal nursery; if it were a setting for a Stephen King novel, it would be *The Shining*.

The cardinals are, of course, doing what comes naturally. They are following a pattern that is dictated by something, I don't dare enter the controversy about what that is. And policy and L–D debaters who march in with their same generics and same tired blow up the world theatrics are stupid cardinals — birdbrains, if you will. (Sorry, I had to. No, I didn't tell the whole story just to get that lame punch line.) In the same way, interpers who take the usual route are boring the judge right out of the nest, and orators and L–Dr's who ignore the fact that the other competitor might have done more thinking than they have is asking to be eaten. (I dunno. You think I flogged that metaphor to death yet?)

D. Let me give you a sample affirmative on the Ultimate Topic in a lame brain style. Yeah, I just dreamed it up. But I assure you the evidence is good. (Verrry Good. Just ask for it after the round, when its too late.)

Observation: Slugs threaten world peace

Scenario one: World leaders, sitting nervously in conference, are revolted by a slug crawling onto the conference table. As each vie for the pleasure of grabbing the salt shaker and watching the demise of the disgusting thing, a dispute breaks out. Nuclear War!

Scenario two: As we all know, young students are doing poorly in school, threatening the security of all present and future generations. Old research believed that these students were merely dreaming about dinosaurs. Nay! It is fear of suddenly having a slug crawl out of the ear of their teacher that is causing those vacant stares and falling grades.

Plan: A world wide program to sprinkle salt on slugs will begin immediately.

Advantage: removal of slugs will be feasible, fun and impossible for the negative to find evidence about, until we change this case to copperhead snakes next week!

Underview: anything that increases world security should be adopted.

E. Exercise the Nine. Map the case above.

F. Now, assuming you are a well trained, a.k.a. brainwashed debater, you already think you have the arguments that will, er, nuke this case. You are thinking "T" or "J" or "B.S." De Bono calls your thinking about this case *vertical thinking*. Vertical thinking is evaluative thinking; it takes an idea and subjects it to criticism until it stands approved or defeated. It is thinking the usual, predictable way; it's reaching for the generics and the counterplan, because by golly, we did it fifteen times already and it's never lost yet.

Vertical thinking is the bread and butter of most forensics events. That huge file box of yours is an altar to the glory of vertical thinking. Here, says the ox-box, is the Ark of the Covenant. Buy this handbook, attend this camp, and thee shalt never toil with thy brain again.

Yeah? You're my meat.

The beauty of this "weak" case is that it is impervious to the usual argument. Of course, being brainwashed, you don't understand that this case has already been buttressed against the usual generic disad attack.

G. The parts of an argument, Part eight- the criteria/pre-empt

An argument, as you will remember, is like a house. Of course, if you want a cold draft house, you build it on a hill. But if you want a snug, warm home, free from those chilly Malthus d/a's, you need a buttress.

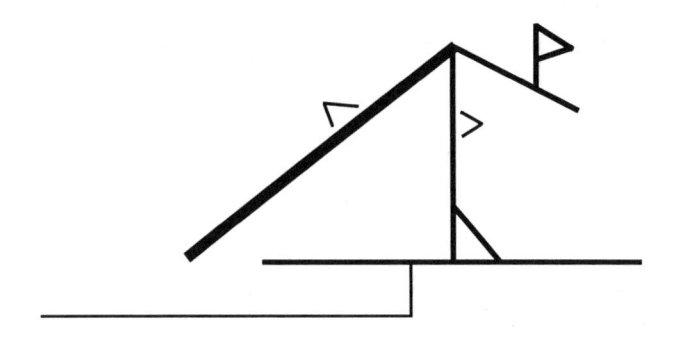

H. The buttress forces the other side into a position. Unfortunately for the attacker, to coin a phrase, the choices are Dumb and Dumber. In the example above, the attacker must either agree with the criteria, or specifically attack it.

I. Dumb. If the attacker agrees with the underview, or just doesn't get to it in the 1NC because he is too busy with a three minute topicality spew, the affirmative has the debate cold. Time element is on the affirmative side, and the "we blow up the world first" argument usually beats the "yeah, but we blew it up seven times" argument. Once the decison rule underview is adopted, all that remains is mopping up.

J. Dumber. Attacking the criteria straight up places the attacker on the strongest affirmative ground. "Nuke war is good" is a ridiculous argument that only wins when the affirmative is Dumbest. This is a shaky proposition as the presence of a criteria should be your fair warning that you don't have two bozos on the other team.

So, you say, counter-plan. Also, fine with me. The presence of the criteria has made competitiveness very difficult to prove.

K. Are you still arguing with me? Are you still saying — but I have evidence that says... !? I repeat — you're my meat. All I have to do is hear that argument once, and recognize it as your only defense. You are a cardinal, returning to the Bates Honeysuckle Motel. Avoid the shower, please.

L. The opposite of vertical thinking is *lateral thinking*. Lateral thinking is not evaluative. Lateral thinking is an idea generating machine that eventually produces the seeds for argument that, when run through the vertical

Where The Good Arguments Are

thinking mill, produces a devastating argument. In truth, all the great generic d/a's began with lateral thinking. Some debaters sat around in rooms filled with hallucinogens and tried to come up with something "they'll never think of." And they did — I was in on the development of one of the first "growth" d/a's. These arguments were extrememly successful. Then, they became scripture, and they entered vertical thinking hell. Now, the only way you can win a growth disad is if your opponents don't have the money to buy the handbooks.

M. Homework — Here is an opening technique. I want you to spend at least a half hour employing to come up with a list of arguments to attack the slug case. DeBono calls it the PMI.

PMI stands for *Positives, Negatives,* and *Interesting.* I'll start you with an opening statement: "Slugs are disgusting."

N. Alternate homework for other events

    1. Extempers, do a PMI on:
       The Presidency is an outdated institution in the late twentieth century.

    2. Orators and L–D'ers, do a PMI on:
       Honesty as a virtue is dead.

    3. Interpers, do a PMI on:
       The face is more powerful than the voice.

O. Don't cheat yourself. Do it right. It was a short lesson. I asked you to learn today, but the results of your homework should bring a jolt to your heart and an evil smile to your lips. And then you'll know what Geoff Goodman knew back in the seventies.

Or did he...?

Chapter Six

I punched up Mr. Goodman's home number. A woman answered. Panic! Hang up! Huh? No, go ahead and talk, you idjit!

-No, Geoff's not here. He's an assistant district attorney here in Sacramento. He has a trial and he is overpreparing, as usual.

Geoff Goodman has to prepare? It must be true what my students say — you must get stupider as you get older.

-Er, does he still have, well, great big hair?

-No, he's a prosecutor now. But it's still very curly.

-Oh.

-Look, give me your number and I'll have him call you.

-Oh, no, don't do that. I'm the one wanting to bother him, so-

-No, it's all right. Give me your number.

You ever just sat around waiting for Einstein to call?

Po' Li'l Me

A. Examining the homework
B. Vertical versus lateral thinking revealed
C. Arguments off lateral thinking
D. Arguments off both sides of an Interesting idea.
E. The Dominant Idea
F. Exercise 10
G. The Critical Factor
H. The best alternative
I. The Dominant Ideas of events
J. Po
K. Exercise 11
L. Mr. Schofield reveals the process
M. The Dominant Idea on the Old China Topic
N. The follow up question
O. Vertical thinking redux
P. Homework
Q. Analysis of your current topic
R. A P.S. 4 L–D

"There may not be a reason for saying something until after it has been said"

— Edward de Bono, *de Bono's Thinking Course*

A. You should have two sets of homework that we haven't examined yet: 4-O,P and 5-M,N. Get those out and review them. If you didn't do them, welcome to the ignorant late twentieth century. I can't help you. Go play vertically for a while. It's all you do well. ("Here's a quarter. Go call your mother and tell her you'll never be a thinker." Ooooh, I always wanted to say that.)

B. For you hard workers, what do you see? If you absorbed Chapter Five, you can see that your arguments against the slug case are vertical thinking; the case says X, and you say not X. Even when you Engulf and Devour, it's in a predictable manner. After all, the ultimate vertical thinking is "case outweighs." There is nothing ravenous about that.

C. Now, take a look at the list of ideas you generated on "slugs are disgusting." This list of concepts is the outgrowth of lateral thinking. There has to be the germ of a few good arguments in there. Think how your opponents will react when you run them. Even more incredible, consider what your arguments could be like after you practice lateral thinking and develop more mental muscle. Now we should begin to map your best ideas and develop them vertically. Let's take an example, just to open a few vistas.

D. In my list of interesting ideas, appears this — who says that slugs are disgusting? I wager it is the shallow, the uninformed, the sans-culottes of the nature world! To give in to this speciesism is exactly the wrong solution!

E. Let's explore lateral thinking much more, beginning with what hampers competitors from using it. The first limitation is called the Dominant Idea.

The Dominant Idea is what gives the vertical thinking pattern its rigidity. Take your parents (please! Thank you, Henny!). For many of us martyrs who find ourselves parents at advanced ages, the dominant idea is that the parent Knows and the child Does Not Know. Therefore, whenever the Dominant Idea is present, alternatives that can be considered against it will be scarce, even when I am being "open minded." This is bad, because if I am considering this as a problem, it is probably the Dominant Idea which is either the source of the difficulty, or the reason why I cannot solve it.

This is such an important concept let me tell you of a problem at my high school. On Prom Night, a couple of dozen kids rented a school bus as their limo. (Cute idea!) The problem was they installed a cooler of booze on the bus. You might think this is also a cool idea, but there we must part company.

Now my school has a black eye, because the incident hit the newspapers. We look like a bunch of ... enough. But the discussions of solutions are dominated by a polarity — those who think stronger measures are needed to avoid more incidents, and those who argue that limitations do not punish the guilty, but the innocent (most on the bus were seniors).

F. Exercise the Now — discover the Dominant Idea of the Prom.

G. Sometimes the Dominant Idea is difficult to discover. The formulation of the Dominant Idea into definable terms is critical, because otherwise we will still be unable to escape it. Therefore, we look for the glue which holds the Dominant Idea together, (the second inhibitor of lateral thinking) and that is called the Critical Factor.

Though like a competent detective I'm sure you have discovered the Dominant Idea of the Prom, let's assume we are still stumped in putting it into words. Therefore, we look for the Critical Factor of the Prom. What is it that makes the Prom such a huge emotional, rebellious event, and therefore such a source of conflict? I can suggest to you many less than critical factors — the high expectations, the money that has been swept away in formal wear and other artificial expenses and more. But the Critical Factor that strikes me is this — the Prom is "playing sophisticated adult." Maybe you disagree with me, but the test is this — if the Critical Factor is removed, does the Dominant Idea become clear or even irrelevant? I think it does; therefore the Dominant Idea of the Prom is Rite of Passage. Margaret Mead would nod in agreement — in a world of artificial growing up, and with a desperate lack of rites of passage of substance for teenagers, America has substituted the Prom.

H. What's the point, Old Man, besides the fact that you had a couple of lousy prom dates, and you're bitter? We can now proceed to use lateral thinking to find a solution to our problem of drinking at the Prom. If the Dominant Idea is so critical that a successful Prom MUST be a rite of passage, then we can begin with a PMI on the statement "The Rite of Passage must be of worth." If we want to remove the Dominant Idea, we can begin with a PMI on 'The Rite of Passage concept is irrelevant to the Prom."

Until we have removed the gagging restrictions of vertical thinking, even the ideas upon which the vertical thinking is based, we will never find the best alternative.

Now, if you please, solve our problem of the Prom and drinking. I think that you will find some solutions that will startle you —"I came up with that?"

I. Now let's turn our attention back to the events that brought you to the dance (sorry!). What Dominant Ideas limit us in considering these events in a new light?

   1. What limits extemp? What makes it increasingly the same? The dominant idea of extemp has become the quotation. If we are looking to make a breakthrough in extemp, let's explore what the event would be like without that Dominant Idea.

   2. What is the Dominant Idea of the Interps? I think I can easily identify a Critical factor in Interp — every DI is an emotional rollercoaster but not very dramatic, and every HI is frantic, noisy and usually not very funny. I'm sorry to seem the cynic, but you ought to have to judge the interps once in a while. Often it is not a pleasant experience at all, even in elims. Why is that? Must it be that way?

   3. The Dominant Idea in Oratory? Could a Critical Factor be only a fool takes chances with the mindset of the judge?

   4. Why is L–D the most unpredictable of all the events? Is it a case of an event without a Dominant Idea?

J. To remove a Dominant Idea so as to begin lateral thinking, use the concept which DeBono calls "po." Po stands for Provocative Operation, and when used it describes a concept that runs against reality for the main purpose of releasing the mind for lateral thinking. A student came to me moaning about his lack of success with the opposite sex. It proved too much to discuss why "Jack is a loser with women." But the po concept leads us to "Po Jacks are successful with women." After some lateral thinking and a couple of PMI's, we had an interesting idea or sixteen. I tore up the Minuses and gave him the lists of the Positives and Interestings. The result was a list of ideas where Jack could cease being a Neanderthal and begin concrete operations at the Cro-Magnon stage. He still doesn't have a girlfriend, but at least they've stopped burning him in effigy.

Some po examples from our area of discussion ;
  Po slugs are cute and cuddly.
  Po Interps are quiet and intimate.
  Po Oratories are deep philosophical treatises.
  Po tournaments are relaxed and non-competitive.

Now, describe what qualities these Po objects have, and explore reasons why.

K. Exercise the Absolutely Now

1. Po extemp is not an exercise in memorization. What is it instead?

2. Po interp is described by theatre buffs as 'powerful actor's training'. How does it gain this reputation?

3. Po oratory is often published by newspapers as editorial. Why?

4. Po L–D is now used as the format in presidential campaign debates. Why do thoughtful citizens endorse it?

5. Po policy debate doesn't use flow sheets. In fact, all notetaking is banned. Why?

L. Remember my conversation with King Schofield? This is how Mr. Schofield described the approach that they used on most affirmative cases.

"We liked to run inherency in the 1NC. This forced the affirmative to declare why things are structured the way they are. When they responded, Geoff would show why those answers would still destroy the solvency of the affirmative plan."

"We liked to run it on the East Coast teams with Midwest judges. Of course, it probably wouldn't work anymore, since judges won't buy inherency as a voting issue anymore."

Now you can give a name to what Mr. Goodman and Mr. Schofield did. Do you agree that it won't work anymore? Of course, many teams today try to trade-off disads in both directions, but that is a vertical approach that gives no flexibility to your argument. Run the trade-off disads long enough, and the entire circuit gets wise. Then you have to buy a new set of handbooks. (Remember Clinton good - Clinton bad?) That isn't debating — that's avoidance.

But running inherency is not the only way to make an affirmative commit to a Dominant Idea. Mr. Goodman and Mr. Schofield didn't have cross-ex back when dinosaurs ruled the Earth, so they had to run the inherency arguments to get the affirmative to commit. Now, a few well placed questions, the best one of which is 'why?', will do the job for you.

M. Removing the Dominant Idea on China. An old topic, but a good one to demonstrate this concept. Let's say you meet one of those teams who take advantage of the college judge(c/j). They refuse to give an inherency argument, because they know that the c/j is unlikely to vote on it. Then they refuse to answer questions in c/x, since the c/j is out getting lung cancer anyway. (Yes, I'm being unfair. Almost all college judges view a debate with an open mind. But that mind usually follows an absolute vertical pattern — to run certain arguments is not only ineffective, but you may lose merely because you run them. Every person in the United States should judge debates. No judge is ever better than another. But I think that a restricted style of debate is unfair to the debaters and bad for the future of high school debate — what little it has left. Thank you, I feel better now.)

So, the time has arrived to play the advantage against itself. Let's say the affirmative claims that U.S. pressure on the spread of nuclear technology will stop China from selling necessary equipment to build the bomb to renegade nations.

In C/X, ask "I'm confused. Tell me how the solvency mechanism works." The affirmative, with a smile on her lips, and a sneer in her heart, will tell you. In essence, she will claim that the U.S. has great influence over China.

N. Follow up: "Did your evidence give that analysis?"

Answer – Yes. That's fine, the affirmative has now committed itself to inherency as clearly as if they had run it themselves. Now, if you run your arguments based on that mechanism, the affirmative can't deny it as proven. To read more evidence would be redundant.

Other answer – No. This is more fun. Ask the affirmative if you can stipulate (that is, both sides agree as fact) the solvency mechanism. The affirmative had better say yes. Then run your arguments. When the affirmative says "no evidence," shake your head in amazement — the affirmative already agreed to it. But if cross- ex is not binding, then the affirmative immediately must read a quote proving the analysis of the solvency mechanism, else they lose.

What are the arguments? I ask you. Don't you just hate having to think?

Last thought — get the affirmative to stipulate that the Chinese are reasonable. Obviously, if the Chinese are bonkers, trying to manipulate them is useless. But if they are reasonable, I would argue all you have to do is find the reasonable alternative, and the Chinese will take it. There is no need for evidence — the affirmative has granted it.

O. You say that affirmatives don't have to do that? You old vertical thinker you. That's precisely the reason why high school policy debates end with both sides telling each other what they don't have to do. The judge then winds up making a decision on what he is told he cannot do. Has that happened to you? Then make sure you do the next exercise carefully.

P. Exercise the Future (for all but policy debate) — what do the Po's tell you about why events have evolved to their present status? What ideas do you have to escape the problems that these Dominant Ideas have given each event? Why would an escape from the dominant idea be a refreshing change?

Q. Policy debate exercise — Take your current topic and determine the Dominant Idea. Apply this to five affirmative case areas. Chortle. How this will amaze and depress your opponents.

R. A postscript for L–Dr's. you probably know that your event was created in reaction to the Dominant Idea of policy debate. What impact has this fact had on the development of a Dominant Idea for Lincoln–Douglas?

Chapter Seven

–Hello, is this Bill Davis? I'm Geoff Goodman.

–Be still my beating heart! (What a stupid thing to say!)

Mr. Goodman talks me through my problem.

–A process? No, just lots of advance preparation. We'd talk about what the case might be, and where the debate might go. Then it just went.

– But... where did the arguments come from?

–The germ of them was in the advance preparation. Then the arguments were just there.

– But – did you ever go dry?

–Oh, yes. Lots of times.

But if Geoff Goodman didn't know how he did it, how those fresh sparkling arguments arrived and spilled persuasively into the round, well then... ah, maybe it's just talent. Some things you just can't explain.

It wasn't until hours later that I realized that he had told me the secret very precisely.

More Exercises than Jane Fonda

A. Hard work awaits
B. Exercise 12
C. Exercise 13
D. Exercise 14
E. Attacking yourself - the source of true paranoia
F. The origin of arguments
G. Ideas on the other events
H. Homework
I. For advanced learners

"The imagination may be compared to Adam's dream- he awoke and found it truth."

-Keats

A. To find the truth, I'm gonna work you to death. By the time you're done with this lesson, the exercises should prove to you that you can be a better debater, extemper, interper or orator by using argument mapping and/or lateral thinking.

B. Exercise Twelve (for everyone) – Go back and re-read the essay that began Chapter One.

   1. Map it. All of it.

   2. Discover the Dominant Idea.

   3. Attack the essay, using every tool you have learned. Write it all down. Don't fool yourself by nodding your head and forgetting what you have discovered. You must see it to be able to claim it.

C. Exercise Thirteen (should I skip this number?) – for each event

   1. Policy debate – I have run against you an affirmative that subjects all juvenile offenders to shock treatments. Map it. Discover the Dominant Idea. Use lateral thinking to discover a competing idea, and use it to destroy the affirmative.

   2. Extempers, L–Dr's and orators – "TV causes violence in children." Create the argument, then map it, discover the Dominant Idea, and prepare a speech attacking the statement.

   3. Interpers – go dig up the balcony scene from *Romeo and Juliet*. Map Juliet's "arguments." Discover the Dominant Idea. Now, re-examine the scene with a new Dominant Idea inserted .

D. Exercise Fourteen – Back to the Truth. If you haven't done Exercise One yet, stop and go do it.

It would be stupid for me to say I can give you "the answers" to Exercise One. There are so many potential arguments that I couldn't ever begin to cover them. Also, the arguments that you discovered using lateral thinking are unique to you; I could never come up with them without your help.

But what I can do is give you a list of arguments that I discovered. You try to identify how I came up with those arguments. Then, below, I have listed the areas of the argument map(s) that created the arguments, and the Interesting Ideas that spawned them after I had done three PMI's.

E. Schizophrenia – attacking my own argument.

   1. The essay never defines Truth. If Truth lies only in reality, and not within the individual, then the reading of evidence is all that is necessary to move towards it. What the individual

More Exercises than Jane Fonda

debater believes is not only irrelevant, it gets in the way of the Truth.

But if Truth lies within the individual, then all the essay can attack is that debaters run arguments that the author believes are insincere. This is none of the author's business. Further, if Truth lies within the individual, it is up to the judge to suspend her views of the Truth so that she can evaluate the arguments of the debaters.

2. The essay attacks debaters because they do not do what the format does not allow them to do. The author does not present any evidence that failing to find the Truth is a) possible in a debate format, no matter what the intents of the debater or b) desirable. If the Truth is discoverable within a debate, then the side which is granted the Truth by the side of the topic they happen to be assigned would win the debate by default. Therefore, to attack the lack of Truth in a debate is like executing the doctor because the patient died of an incurable disease.

3. The essay never proves that cases with high truth values actually are more successful than those based on wild flights of fancy. The fact that three affirmative cases did well on the immigration topic is a testimony to the skills of the debaters, not to the affirmative cases.

4. But let us assume that the author is correct, and the purpose of debate is to discover Truth. There is no guarantee that this will make debaters more lovable. I seem to remember a few martyrs in history who died for telling the Truth.

5. And if the author truly believes in his argument, he must change the concept of judging debate from one of attempting to be precise and therefore fair (i.e. the policy maker paradigm) to judging based on a nebulous concept that cannot be defined except when the judge claims she

sees it. (I can't define pornography, but I can tell you when I see it). This is not progress.

6. The author throws out the baby with the bathwater. Great debates occur all the time. Just because he saw a few bad ones does not mean that the activity is worthless without his wisdom.

F. Here's where my arguments originated in the argument map and in the interesting columns of the PMIs

Argument #	Argument Map	Interesting Idea
1	definitions	What is Truth? Where is it?
2	assumptions	Does the format allow for the T?
3	evidence	What affects a debate the most – the arguments or the debaters?
4	Engulf and Devour	Is T necessarily a good thing?
5	implications	Is T practical as a basis for judging?
6	assumptions	Dominant idea is the debate ill.

G. The other exercises:

1. Policy debate – some attacks. Please compare to your own, and identify where I found each of them.

    A. The Dominant Idea of the affirmative on shock treatment of juveniles claims that crime is a mental disorder. This not only isn't true, but has scary implications if it would be. We must give all criminals shock treatment. To only shock the young would

More Exercises than Jane Fonda   171

somehow make their acts different than that of adults, and the Dominant Idea is that crime is deviant.

B. Where is the line of deviancy in crime? Murder is pretty deviant, but what about drug abuse? Speeding? Jaywalking? Tearing the tags off mattresses?

C. If crime is mental, what event causes the criminal to veer off the straight and narrow? If there is one, shouldn't we work to remove that event? Or, if it's genetic, how will a jolt of juice change the behavior?

D. Final implication, for the grins. Whoever loses this debate should get zapped, since to lose a debate is to say you lied, and that's deviant.

2. Extempers, L–Dr's and Orators — My argument map in favor of the argument.

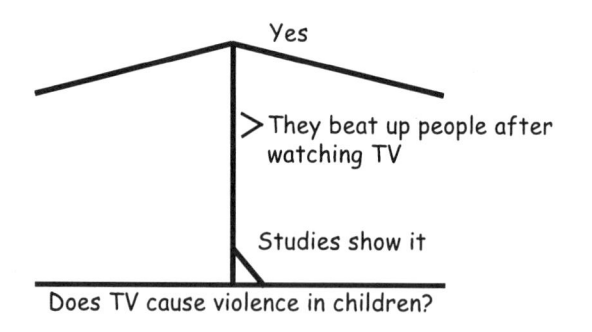

```
                    Yes
         _____|_____
        /           |           \
                    | > They beat up people after
                    |   watching TV
                    |
                    | Studies show it
        _____|_____
           Does TV cause violence in children?
```

My map against the argument.

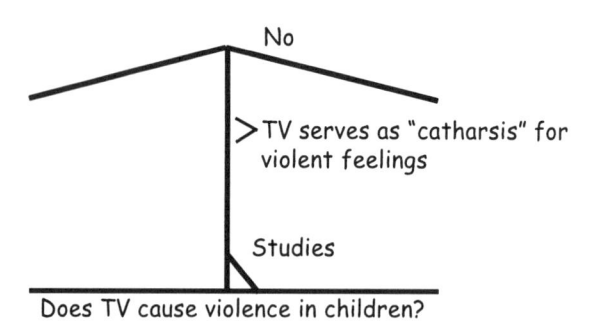

```
                    No
         _____|_____
        /           |           \
                    | > TV serves as "catharsis" for
                    |   violent feelings
                    |
                    | Studies
        _____|_____
           Does TV cause violence in children?
```

172 A Tool For Forensics — Critical Thinking and Lateral Thinking

Now here is the critical step, and why argument mapping is so useful for the speaking events. This is now my thesis.

For the issue: TV fosters violence in children by showing them violence, not only in regular programming, but in cartoons as well.

Against the issue: Not only is TV not the source of violence in children, as the widespread violence in society in general shows, but TV may actually reduce violence due to its cathartic effect.

3. Interpers — the Dominant Idea of the balcony scene on first reading seems to be true love discovered. But what if you had a different Dominant Idea? Franco Zefferelli's idea in his famous movie was sexual — both R &J wanted it, and the only thing stopping them was their youth and fear of getting caught. How about the balcony scene as teenage rebellion? Look how that would change the delivery (interpretation) of the lines. For a feminist perspective, try the Dominant Idea as manipulation of women by men.

   Next look at the assumptions of Juliet's lines. From my male perspective, they pretty clearly show that sweet Juliet is a tease. A more forgiving female friend says that the assumptions show Juliet's pure innocence. Either interpretation works, and both can be moving.

H. Is for Homework. Go back to the Alpha etc. arguments from Lesson two. review them. PMI them. Discover the Dominant Idea and the Critical Factors. Meditate for a while on how far you have come. Next we will discover how to better construct arguments. One more to go — hang in there!

I. If you really think you understand the lessons, rewrite the essay on debate and truth to pre-empt the arguments that you have devised against it. Or, if you really think you're tough, write the argument in favor of the best course of action to deal with drinking at the Prom.

More Exercises than Jane Fonda

Chapter Eight

- Well, is there anything that you have learned from practicing law that you wish you'd known while you were debating?

- Hmm. No, not really. The law has taught me always to focus on what's important. Do everything to emphasize your thesis, and avoid what detracts. But I knew that when I was debating.

-How did you know that?

-I learned it (the old fashioned way?).

Building the Perfect Beast

A. Offense over defense?
B. Exercise 15
C. The debate technique learned from mapping.
D. Advice for other speaking events
E. Argument maps and interp.
F. A return to the truth
G. The dialectic
H. L–D'rs- eager learners in the dialectic
I. Oratory and the dialectic
J. Is the theory of the dialectic true?
K. Exercise 16
L. Interp and the dialectic
M. Extemp and the dialectic
N. Debate, the Truth, and the Future
O. Homework?

"Love Truth, but pardon Error"
-Voltaire

A. We have developed an approach that can be extremely effective in shaping a successful approach to forensics. But the problem is, as with war, that any breakthrough in offensive weapons must be mirrored by the defense, else the balance of power is destroyed. Therefore, we need to determine how to build better arguments so that an opponent will have to beware of traps.

B. Exercise Fifteen – review what you learned about argument mapping. What do the techniques prove are unwise approaches to take in building an argument?

C. Here are my answers.

1. Simplicity rules. A case with too many reasons will have too many assumptions. An L–D case with two values, or three criteria, suffers from the same. If argument maps prove anything, it is that each new reason for an argument creates a whole new set of baggage.

2. Evidence is the safest part of an argument. When assumptions or implications fall, so does the argument. When reasons fall, the argument gets shaky. But falling evidence normally does not spell doom for an argument — unless it is really bad. Therefore, for a stronger argument, claim less reasons, read more evidence.

3. Overclaiming is death on an argument. A wise opponent allows the overclaim, and then Engulfs and Devours you. Fight the rush to blow up the world — a few million babies are harm enough to claim a ballot. Even a value advantage in the absence of any disadvantage clearly wins the debate.

4. Policy debaters should run criteria for evaluating decisions, just as L–Dr's do. Some already do so, and call them decision rules. However, I use criteria as a means of protecting the argument — there are many attacks that can be deflected just by the criteria itself.

5. ALWAYS force the opposition to support an argument also. This allows you to Engulf and Devour him, which is the best offensive strategy invented. If the opposition refuses to endorse a position ("all we have

to do is attack the affirmative") de facto end the debate by pointing out that only the affirmative can meet the criteria that the judge should use to decide the debate. This usually gets the opponent pretty stirred up right quick.

D. Of course, extempers and orators will tell you that arguments spread too thin lose judges also. In each of those events, a single reason that reacts negatively on the judge will result in the loss of several ranks. Therefore, follow this advice, if you please.

   1. Evidence everything. The best evidence is often a story. Tell many.

   2. Expose the assumptions of your argument, and then defend them.

   3. The most common "silent objection" that judges have are on the implications of your argument. Anticipate and answer.

   4. Argument maps provide superior thesis statements.

E. Interpers also have much to learn from argument maps. The spoken lines of the character are the reasons, and the subtext provides the assumptions. The key is to sense this tension and sell it with the character.

F. But now we end where we began — the Truth. Even now, I must argue with you that the best arguments will reflect reality as closely as possible. The Johari Window tells us, of course, that we can never see all the Truth. But it also clearly shows that by discovering as many different viewpoints as possible, we can get, we will be closer to the Truth than the person who stops when she finds a view that she believes will "win."

G. The process of coming closer to the Truth is called the dialectic. Hegel, the philosopher, theorized that to each thesis arises its opponent, the antithesis. These two clash and out of the ruins comes a new synthesis, which is the combination of the best parts of both its progenitors. Once established, the synthesis is transformed into the thesis, and a new antithesis arises. Though the dialectic may never bring us the whole Truth, it inevitably moves us closer, as the antithesis takes longer to arise, and arguing in favor of it becomes increasingly difficult.

H. Of course, L–Dr's are familiar with the dialectic — it is the process of this event, after all. But the other events often forget the dialectic, as if they have reached truth and could not become more "realistic." The result is a boring performance.

I. Example – oratory. Take the touchy/feely warm fuzzy be-a-better-you oratory of the eighties. We have largely left this behind in the early break rounds — the subjects sound selfish and trite to our ears. This is not to say we have discovered the Truth in the nineties — all it takes is a round full of sterile oratory to convince you of that. But what oratory awaits is a new antithesis — a challenge to the established order. (Here is a thought — could that antithesis be a style that combines oratory with interp?)

J. But, you say (don't call me by my wife's pet names) how do we know we are coming closer to the truth and not further away? For example, you may attempt to hoist me upon my own petard, and say my views are from a thesis of the seventies, like the origin of my hero. And your criticism is valid — only to the extent that when your antithesis meets my thesis, that you defeat me utterly. And, though that may someday happen, I believe in open discussion that my thesis will do very well, thank you; though it's not the Truth, it contains much of it.

Critics of Hegel show the age of Adolf Hitler as proof of the falsity of the dialectic. After all, if history is one giant stride after another towards the Truth, how could Hitler, the monster of evil, have seemed to portray the Truth to so many?

The possible answer may be that the antithesis posed by the Nazi belief was necessary to demonstrate the necessary destruction of hatred on basis of race or religion. This is not to say that this synthesis is obvious to all in the world, because the common genocides continue. But many millions now see this necessary point than understood it before the cataclysm we call the Holocaust.

K. Exercise Sixteen (the last) – Map J. and attack it.

L. Example – interps are the best when they "tell the truth." There was an essay, actually a rave review in the *New Yorker* about the new production of *Hamlet* starring Ralph Fiennes. The review said that Fiennes portrayed the "truest" Hamlet yet, because he had learned his lessons from Olivier, Barrymore and (gulp!) Gibson. The Fiennes Hamlet was an interpretation that truly combined all of the famous predecessors into one. And certainly, concluded the critic, Fiennes was certainly closer than anyone who had refused to try anything new.

Oh, yes, if you accept the theory of the dialectic, it applies to you in any event you choose. And the best way to discover the truth is by unlimited alternatives, then analysis of their strengths and weaknesses.

You now have the tools to do it.

M. Extempers, the dialectic is your key to avoiding the devastating ranking that proves you have done something to anger the judge. As a person who has suffered quite a few ignorant speeches, the Rush Limbaughs of the extemp genre, I can assure you that the dialectic is the key to excellent extemp. By finding and adopting the synthesis, the judge who may hold to the thesis or antithesis will find something in your work to please her, regardless of her beliefs.

Therefore, "to thine Truth be True" sayeth this Polonius (and I'll stay away from wall tapestries).

N. And last and never least, debate, sweet argument, my love. I would like to think that all of us who follow your muse would practice your virtues. But we don't, it's obvious. Perhaps we will never be able to reconcile a desire for victory with a synthesis that brings all of us closer to the truth. Yet I can testify that the search for synthesis has been a strategy that has served my debaters well, and possibly that is all that is needed to create a new dialectic.

O. Homework. Practice. Perform well. And avoid the cheap win. A thought for a PMI: Po Victory loves honor.

Someday we'll discuss it. Laterally, of course.

Epilogue

– But when will you enter politics?

– I worked for the legislature for awhile, but I don't have any political ambitions. My wife is the politician in the family.

–Really?

–Yeah. She's on the school board.

And it fits. It really does. My debate archetype continues to do what he did even then — prepare, think, and surprise anyone who has the temerity to try to predict him.

No matter what else my faults, I pick my heroes well.

Pot Pourers

Gomer

(originally published 1995)

Buzz. Hey Buzz. Wake up.

Umph? Huh? Where am I?

The Rest-Inn, Buzz. With your good buddy, Gomer. Remember?

Oh, so it wasn't a nightmare.

Huh? Whatcha mean, Buzz?

Nothin' Gomer. What's eatin' you, good buddy?

How'd you know I'm upset?

Oh, maybe the fact the lights are on, and the toilet is runnin', and you're pacing on top of the beds.

Yeah? Oh, I'm sorry, Buzz. Did it hurt?

I have no immediate marriage plans, so I guess there's no damage done. Get down. There. Now, what is it?

Well, Buzz, I guess you remember, I got eliminated from the tournament today.

I seem to remember that.

And maybe you don't know, but this was my last tournament of my career, at least in high school.

Well, I'm sure the colleges will be interested in you...

You think so? You think they want somebody who never won a single tournament in four years?

Why not?

Or someone who never broke into elims in four years?

There are lots of schools out there. . .

Or someone who never won a single debate in four years?

Um-well now. . .

No, Buzz, tell me straight.

Prolly not, Gomer. But that's no big deal.

It's not? I went to sixteen tournaments each year for four years. I never won a single debate, not even to Bye. In the dictionary, my picture is next to loser. What was it all for?

Well, think of all the people that you made happy.

Thanks, Buzz. Thanks a lot.

All right, that was uncalled for. But — pass me that flat stale cola drink over there. (Notice to Coke and Pepsi; your name here! Cheep!) Ah, I'm now ready to become Philosophy Man!

Wow! No wonder you win every L–D tournament, Buzz — um, I mean Philosophy Man!

That's right. I have read every significant philosophical document from Plato to Cato, from Paul's to Rawls', and from Cobain to novocaine.

Jeepers. My little philosophy problem of severe depression due to Terminal Losing will be easy for you, huh!

Well, not really. You have a special case.

I knew it!

It's a special case because you have lost anonymously. No headlines in the paper. No stories in the ten o'clock news about your losing streak. In fact, Gom, no one but you really knows just how bad you are.

Well, that's good... I think.

Of course it's good. All you have to do is deal with your own attitudes towards it. No one is gonna stick it back into your face.

Yeah. I guess I ought to be grateful. Except I'm not.

I know. So let's see if we can figure exactly what you have accomplished in your career. Let's start someplace, like at the beginning. Why did you decide to debate?

Because my Mom made me. She said anyone who could argue as much as me should do something with it.

Did you ever beat her?

Of course not. What kind of a creep do you think I...

I mean, did you ever debate her?

Yeah. When I wanted to keep on debating every year. She said I was worthless.

And you convinced her otherwise, right?

No, I forged her signature on the enrollment form.

Hmmm. Well, how about Coach? If you're so bad, why did she allow you to come back every year?

You know why, P.M. Can I call you that? I was the only one who would debate with Lester the Molester.

Gomer 185

Ahh, then, why did she let Lester come back every year?

Because he was the only one who would debate with ME! You aren't makin' me feel much better, Buzz.

I can see that. That lamp can't stand much more chewing. Sit down and listen.

All right. But it better be good. I'm about to lick this light socket and end it all.

What's the purpose of education, Gom?

Huh? Whaddya mean?

Why are you here. In this crummy motel? With me?

Uhhh — for the babes?

Wrong! Try again. What brought you back for four years? To keep losing?

Because I thought... I really thought... I would eventually win one...

O.K. Blow your nose on this pillow case. Yours, not mine. But what did you feel like in every debate, before you got that crummy ballot that told you that you lost?

Well, Buzz, lots of times I thought I won.

Exactly. Why?

Because... well... I thought I had done a better job than the other guys. And once in while, when Lester didn't pull the switchblade and threaten the judge, I thought he liked me.

And what did you do to deserve that?

Come again?

Why did you think you should win? That the judge liked you?

Because… I was getting better.

Getting better? How?

Well, I no longer drooled in my rebuttals. And — and I stopped wearing my rubber underwear my senior year… and I hardly ever still needed it.

Exactly. You were learning. And that's what education should be all about!

But I have no proof that I ever learned anything.

Not true. How is learning shown? How do you know anyone has learned anything?

By making them take a test? And if that's it, I flunked every one.

No. You passed. Learning is shown by behavior change — anything less is immeasurable. Could the Gomer of this year have beaten the Gomer of freshman year?

You bet! And the janitor, too!

There you are. You improved tremendously, and you are just as good as the people who beat you. In fact, you're better, because you are a nicer guy, and went a lot farther than some of these honchos who won everything in sight the whole four years.

So you're saying that if I could clearly beat the Gomer of the past with the Gomer of today, that I'm a winner?

Well said. Only the Gomer of today could have said it.

Wow! you're right Buzz, er, Philosophy Man! I feel much better.

Good. Now, climb down off the ceiling and let's get some shut eye.

O.K. You're right. I am a lot better. Jeepers.

Yeah. *quiet now.*

Wow... Buzz?

WHAT!

Where do you think I can debate the Gomer of the Past?

Squad Spirit
or
A Christmas Quarrel

(Originally published December 1992)

And so it came to pass, of all of the good nights of the year, upon District Tournament eve, Screwloose the Coach sat in his class room, meditating on the sins of his squad. He had one student who laughed when other students lost, and two who cried when the first one won, and three who hated four who despised the five who — well, it was just one great big pile of sins.

Suddenly, Screwloose heard a harsh clanking deep down, down in the bowels of the building. At first, he thought it was only the steam pipes, but when the clanking was accompanied by moans of "NO! PLEASE! Don't make me judge policy!" Screwloose knew that spirits do walk the earth. And then the door seemed to melt away, and a ghastly spectre peered inside. The vision groaned and spake! "Pardon me, but is this the coaches' lounge?"

Screwloose knew him. It was the previous coach at the school who had coached for two years but had been paid for twenty. "It can't be," roared Screwloose, "but it must be! It's Gnarly's ghost!"

"Mr. Gnarly to you," retorted the shade, pouring a scalding cup of coffee from Screwloose's thermos, and testing it with a finger. "Ah, ice cold! So much cooler than the place where I come from!" He poured the brew into his gaping mouth, Screwloose goggled as the liquid coursed through the transparent ghost, and then collected in a steaming puddle on a pile of scripts on the floor. Gnarly glanced down and emitted a nasty chuckle. *Agnes of God* again this year, eh, Screwloose? I could give you a few suggestions, but, never mind. I've been sent to warn you."

Screwloose's smile looked as if he was judging humorous interp. "Warn me? You've scared the dickens out of me already."

Gnarly chuckled as he poured coffee on a handbook. "You don't believe in spirit, do you? No, not me. Of course you believe in my existence. Anyone who can send a kid off to a tournament with "The Scarlet Ibis" in DI believes in miracles. No, Screwloose, what you don't believe in is squad spirit. You believe in these kids as just competitors, and not as a team. And it's clear that they don't believe in it either. They are not only in competition with other school, but in competition with each other. They blame each other for their failures. And you know, Screwloose, they blame you."

"Me! What can I do about it?"

"Good, right to cue. I've brought you help. The other day I was wandering through some of the warmer regions of my current domain, and I stumbled across the coaches from eastern Kansas. They were waiting out a Student Congress and the time. To get to the point, I asked them for their suggestions on how they increased spirit on their own squad. Their answers fell into three categories — fellowship, support, and reasonable expectations."

FELLOWSHIP

1. Parties. You knew that. What is unusual is the variety of suggestions:
   a. First of the season football game and cookout.
   b. Pizza party after hosting the tournament.
   c. Christmas party with gag gifts (make sure you set careful parameters).
   d. Initiation (not hazing) for novices on the first overnight.
   e. Crossing the Equator ceremonies upon passing a certain landmark on trips.
   f. All night cut and paste marathon.
   g. Stopping to bowl on the way home from a tournament.
2. Notes on the bulletin board for squad members only.
3. Making the squadroom a home away from home. Encourage the squad members to "hang out" around the room before and after school.
4. Work sessions with pizza brought in.
5. Worknights at somebody's house with recreation breaks, such as ping-pong.
6. Squad T-shirts, with nicknames on the back.
7. An inside joke board with phrases hilarious to squad members only.

8. Keep a scrapbook with photos, news clips and other documents.
9. Have each student write a biography of the career of another student, and "publish" it for all and possibly for others to read later.

SUPPORT

1. Brothers and Sisters-students paired off for mutual support. They help eachother like wake-up calls, listening to performances, etc.
2. Debate families-experienced debaters adopt novices. It's always interesting to see who of a dual male policy debate team gets to be called "Mom."
3. Roll calls with a compliment from one squad member to another as a response. Variations on this theme ("who is your secret hero?") are endless.
4. Have squad members not going to a tournament write a cheer for those departing.
5. Secretly organize the school's cheerleaders and pep band to come crashing into a squad meeting for a surprise pep rally.
6. Squad officers send notes of congratulations to winners.
7. School announcements of winners. There are many variations, but my favorite is a bulletin board outside the room decorated with flashing lights.
8. A spirit chair, who decorates lockers, cars, etc. of competitors.
9. A dinner prepared by novices the night before a big tourney. Program includes practice, then dinner followed by an inspirational movie.
10. A squad song book. Write songs in the van on the way to tournaments, and save them for the year-end party.

REASONABLE EXPECTATIONS

I believe that the biggest threat to squad unity is disappointment. Jump too high; fall too far. Here are some suggestions to keep failure (and success) in hand.

1. Set reasonable goals for every tournament. Make every tournament a success.
2. A bulletin board with awards such as Best First Negative, etc. Even if nobody wins at a tournament, in class on Monday somebody wins.
3. Practiced behavior at tournaments, such as "How to Win."

4. The awards dinner at the end of the year. It's a hassle, the teary good-bye to the seniors establishes a tradition of caring that is invaluable.

Gnarly paused and then grinned. "Yeah, I know all of these suggestions are work, aren't they, Screwloose? All this takes effort."

Screwloose whined. "But this just sounds like having fun. Why should I have to do this? Isn't squad spirit the kids' business?"

"Business! Education is your business. Judging, teaching and driving is but one drop in the comprehensive ocean of your business. Growing together with each other is the very bottom line of your business."

The ghost passed through the door, then his head reappeared through the solid wood.

"God bless us. Even having fun."

Good Grief!

(Originally published 1994)

WELL, maybe you don't believe it, but I really hate the Big Tournaments.

Some people have the mistaken impression that competitive speech and debate is no big deal, since we players are fortunate to keep our failures out of the newspapers even more often than our successes.

But anybody who ever went into the Big Tournaments with a notion that success lay on the other side of a pack of picky peppery judges knows that Losing — which nearly all of the contestants finally accomplish — is just as much of a personal setback as running the wrong way for a touchdown.

The reason is pretty simple. When you finally lose that last round that kills your dream, what is left is grief. Something died.

Oh sure, everyone tells you that competitive speech is no big deal. Your coach and your colleagues ask you to do something that is frankly impossible and possibly unhealthy. We ask you to work on that oratory, or learn to make that character come alive, or spend hours in the musty library all with a driving dream. And then, when the driving dream runs out of gas, we expect you to shrug your shoulders and say " Oh well. It's just a game."

But games cause grief, too. And perhaps it is worse in our game, because there is no scoreboard telling you that you are failing so that you can get prepared, and the axe finally falls outside of the playing field, sometimes in assemblies where there is no place to hide That long walk back to your seat after taking the third place medal — there's no way to practice it. And even if you could — who would want to?

So, let me give you some unwanted advice in lieu of the practice. A few minutes spent reading this might help if you ever lose a dream. Then again, probably not. After all, it's your decision how much this grief affects you. No one else can do it for you.

A FEW OLD SAWS

1. ACKNOWLEDGE THAT THERE WILL BE NO PHYSICAL LOSS. This might be a good focus for meditation during the wait for the assembly. You might not have the focus when the time comes to remember that nobody dies when the results are announced. Fortunately, we don't turn the lions loose when the judges say "thumbs down." Consider — what happens to the losers in the swine judging at the state fair? And you think you have problems!

2. SEE THE REWARDS. I may be perverse, but this works for me. Frankly, not having to work several more months on this crummy debate topic is an advantage. Letting that character go is like getting a mother-in-law out of the house! And just how many times can you make that oratory sound sincere, buddy? And if it's Nationals you're talking about (All you folks obsessed with nats, turn away — but then you aren't reading this anyway, are you? You KNOW you can't lose?) um... well.. I DO have other things to do with a week in June. Don't you?

3. DIFFERENTIATE. This is a two dollar word that means to not take a ballot personally. In this activity, we have the advantage of performing, more in some events than in others, but still, we are not OURSELVES when we are in front of the judges. Try to remember that the judge could really care less who you are, because it would be too stressful to judge if he/she/it did. Therefore, what the judge is evaluating is you in a different masque. Take off the masque after the judging and you are still whole.

4. GIVE YOURSELF SOMETIME, THEN WASH YOUR HANDS. After the big tournament, allow yourself some time to feel rotten! Twenty-four hours, say. Then, go to a movie, or take a music bath, and bid the dead dream good-bye. It's healthier, easier, and every once in a while, a little self pity feels so bad it's easier to remember to avoid it the next time.

5. AND IF IT REALLY HURTS TOO MUCH, DIVERSIFY. If a couple of days have passed and the whipped dog still appears in the morning mirror, then take the hint. You've got too much of yourself tied up in this activity. By no means am I saying you should quit just because losing

hurts. Instead, find some other activities, even competitive ones, that will give you a wider zone of confidence.

Ah, you say, down there in the black hole of despair; I can't do anything else. Pfui, my friend. The fact you could so intensely wish and work for a desired goal proves you have the drive to do other things well, too. I have a friend who, when her efforts fell short of qualifying for nationals by one place THREE YEARS IN A ROW, became a professional storyteller. She says it gives her as much satisfaction as any performance she gave in four years of competition, and what's more, she gets paid for it.

What is most satisfactory is that our activity spins off success in many different ways, much more than a mere sport can. Reflect on this.

In your long pursuit in quest of perfection in the spoken word, what have you learned about poetry of words and phrases? That alone may be enough to open up another episode of your life.

6. AND IF ALL ELSE FAILS, GO DANCING. 'Nuff said.

You Gotta Know the Rules
(previously unpublished)

Now, we all be well bred and raised in the debate and forensic community in Kansas. Most of us come from two- parent homes even with two humans in 'em, and if we don't we got good therapists we can see at K-State. So when this scandal hit, we were amazed. How could this happen here?

I mean, we really do our best to help each other. When the Boss Lady asks, why, we tell her we enjoy resting her foot on our necks. When CR thought he wasn't gettin' nuff respect, why, we made him Chairman for Life. He'll never feel unloved again. We get misty eyed when he starts usin' that beggin' tone when it gets to be tourney time and we be 76 rounds of judgin' short. Yes, we have no judgin', we have no judgin' today, we sing. The look on his face makes us proud.

Look, we're such a considerate community, that when MH and GB decided to get hitched, they did it on the quiet, jess so we all wouldn't have to be inconvenienced by attendin' a big weddin'. They saved MK a bundle on the rental of the hog trough, not to mention how much the pesticides would have cost just for the resepshun. Just compare that to some other states, where people SAY they be engaged, and then nuthin' happens. I say, "Show Me" a better place than Kansas!

Like I said, we have our barnyard products together here. That is why when one of our fearless leaders was accused of destroyin' a sacred Kansas debate document, we couldn't believe it.

He's the Pope. No, he doan teach in no parochial school, but we already had a King, and the Pope has a spiritual quality to him that we admire. He's humble, trustworthy, and brave, and he has a 12 by 15 foot neon sign on his forehead that lights up to say "TRASH ME. OH, PLEASE TRASH ME. THIS SPACE FOR RENT."

And so, we give the Pope what he wants. We know he appreshiates it by the way he says "STOP THAT &%%$#@ WHISPERING. YOU HEAR ME? STOP THAT PLOTTING!" You never met a more genuine man. And maybe that's why he was entrusted with *The Rules*. Only the Pope, the King and the Chump got a copy of *The Rules*, and it has been a constant contention that if anyone should be the custodian of *The Rules*, it should be the Pope.

Now, I don't have the room to tell you about *The Rules* and how they were found, eerily enough, inside a red sweater in the Pope's basement. But such an immaculate reception clearly implies Heavenly Protection, and the reaction of the Pope to this discovery has puzzled many in the coaches community. In fact, DH and SW are very diligent in expressing their concern for *The Rules*, and each time that they have seen the Pope over, say, the past decade, they have inquired after the safety of the sacred document. It worried them that, after a few very impolite responses, the Pope had fallen into a surly silence on the subject. Nacherly, this increased the concern over the document exponentially, which is about the same as "warp factor five, Scotty." And then, tragedy struck.

DH got a letter from a distant location, say, Las Vegas. Now, DH has learned, from his many years as Honcho in a certain Kansas district, that many horrible things come in the mail. For example, there was the time that CB sent her first born son in Parcel Post in an attempt to get an extry fifteen entries in the district debate tourney. And she didn't even need to get pregnant.

But, nothing that he ever got, even from Seaman High School, horrified DH as much. Out from the document flickered a mutilated sheet from *The Rules*. The sheet was otherwise a nonny mouse. DH immediately suspected that the Mob had abducted the Pope and were using him as a Roman Gladiator at Caesar's, but before he could inform the FBI, he found SW on the other line, as pale with horror as one can be long distance. Fearing the worst, they called the Pope, who denied that *The Rules* were in any jeopardy, except from being applied to DH and SW in a way that is clearly illegal in Kansas, because of necessary laws protecting agricultural livestock.

Then, the horror escalated. More bloody excerpts were received, each time from different postmarks, obviously to throw the Postal Service off the trail of the terrorists. Intense efforts to convince the Pope that he should search diligently for his copy of *The Rules* to secure its safety were greeted with Popish behavior that would be shocking in nearly every city in the United States (excepting Wichjitaw).

Now, it's obvious that the King is not behind this crime. Kings do not deface scripture, they approve it. And it can't be the Chump, because he knows eggxatly where his copy of *The Rules* rests, under honor guard from a vicious five-year-old.

So what may we do? Well, as the librarians at the Great Library of Alexandria found to their horror, documents in rare supply must be copied immediately, in numbers great enough to guarantee the survival of the wisdom they contain.

That is why, to save this for humanity, I will copy the document five times, and send it to places of safe haven. If a package comes from Stilwell, Kansas, you will know it's from me. Unless, maybe, its from the Unabomber.

You Gotta Know the Rules

The Forensics Songbook

(Originally published December 1992)

Big D/A's

(To the tune "Glory Days" with apologies to the Boss)
(To be sung with Slamming Briefcases, Clicking Notebooks, and Gently Ruffling Legal Paper)
(*Adagio*, which means with a fleck of spit on the lower lip)

I knew a guy wuz a great debater back in high school.
He could toss those arguments at ya, make you feel like a fool, boy.
Saw him in the judges' lounge he was walkin' in, I was walkin' out.
Went back inside, drank some coffee grounds but all he could talk about
>Those Big D/A's
>The ones claimin' the end of your days.
>Big D/a's
>Structured down to the little a's.
>Big D/a's. Big D/A's.

I knew a gal who could read those big blocks, baby.
Turn all the judge's heads.
She could talk real nice. She could talk real slow
'Til you wouldn't listen to what she said, yeah.
She and her partner — they won state, provin' sweet talkin' pays.
They thought they were great 'til they hit Nats and ran into all them way
>Big D/A's.
>That big ol' pie in the de-bait sky.
>Big D/A's/
>Put de gleam in de college boy eye.
>Big D/a's. Big D/A's.

I went down to the library, thought I would find me a quote.
Trying to find the link to a decision rule, maybe get me a vote, yeah.

It sent me trailin' back, all the logic of the arguments I had before.
Thought I might use some common sense but all I got was the "four."
>Big D/A's.
>Where the environment fries.
>Big D/A's.
>And the whole world dies.
>Big D/A's. Big D/A's.

>All right! (All right, etc.)
>Nuke War! Go Boom! Nuke War! Go Boom!
>All right! Gonna run Malthus now! Let's Groooooow!

What a Terrible Team

(To be sung to the tune of "Wonderful World")
(With apologies to Sam Cooke)
(Published December 1992, originally written when we were debating Latin America)

He don't know much about proliferation.
Thinks bananas will cause mass starvation.
He don't know much about Nicaragua.
Thinks they shoot a lot, don't drink the agua.
But I do know that's he's a fool.
Can't even give a speech without a drool.
What a terrible, terrible team we would be.

He don't know much about de la Madrid.
Says he went there when he was a kid.
Forgets the "B" when he tries to spell debts.
Thinks Costa Rica plays short for the Mets.
And I do know that he'll get the "4"
Even his Mom thinks he's a crashing bore.
What a terrible, terrrible team we would be.

Now don't tell me that's he's an "A" student.
He's got the brains of a flea.
And just because he may be an "A" student, Coach, yeah
Don't mean he can debate with me.

He thinks Duarte is a German painting.
Can't do rebuttals without spitting or fainting.
Thinks a handbook is a bathroom fixture.
Turns the pages and he looks for pictures.
So I know that you may not like me.
But please don't say he's right for me!
(What a terrible team!) What a terrible, terrible team we would be.

A Chronicle of the Plague Year
or
We Have Met Defoe and He is Us

(originally published May 1994)

(Found upon the demolition of the Buffalo Wallow High School, 20 August 3005. This document was wadded up with figures covered with inexplicable numbers, and fragments of script about mythology from a person named Barnes. We submit it as evidence of a cult in Kansas about this time.)

— 15 May 1994

Lord Copeland:

This be the report of the Buffalo Wallow National Forensic League Chapter for the School Year of Our Lord 1993-94:

Coach, Sponsor, Philosopher, and Friend: Abbott Tublard

Policy debate teams: Brother and Sister Clinton and Clinton, Brother and Sister Aetna and Cigna, and Acolytes Goodman and Musgrave

Value Debaters: Brother Lincoln, Brother Douglas, and Acolyte Crisco

Humorous Interpers: Brothers Moe, Larry and Curly and Sister Whoopi

Dramatic Interpers: Sister Agnes and Brother Brother

Original Oratory: Brother Webster, Brother Clay, and Brother Biden

International extemp: Sister Thatcher, Sister Gandhi and Brother Castro

Student Congress: Sisters Dasher, Dancer, Comet, Cupid, and Vixen

Here are the events of our year. Abbott Tublard says this is the most successful year in Buffalo Wallow High School history! (MiLord, as you know, in Kansas the first semester is dedicated to policy debate, and the other events are performed in the second semester - Abbott Tublard)

August 6, 1993: Brother Clinton finally arrived in Washington for the debate camp that we had faithfully washed cars, trucks, and pigs to raise money for him to attend. Due to some bad luck hitchhiking on the Pennsylvania Turnpike, Brother Clinton arrived without the evidence he had patiently clipped out of the Buffalo Wallow Tribune. He also had lost his clothes. He was greeted in a friendly manner by his roommate from New York: "I see the Tornado. Where's Dorothy?"

August 7: Brother Clinton leaves the debate camp after posting bail with the rest of our money after being charged with assault.

August 21: Abbott Tublard finishes his in-depth preparation for the health care topic by renting and watching "Nurses in Chains" from the B.W. Video and Convenience Store.

August 25: The Tribune concludes it's thirty page Back to School and Football Season supplement with its usual in-depth interview with Abbott Tublard; "We plan to have an educational experience."

August 31: Classes begin! Abbott Tublard gives us the usual pep talk and in-depth topic analysis and sends us to the media center. Brother Aetna quickly checks out the book.

Sept 5: Debate clinic at Kaw State University. The squad thoroughly enjoyed the demonstration debate by the college debaters. They look forward eagerly to the translation promised by mail.

Sept 12: The all night cut and paste marathon is a resounding success. The quote is ready!

Sept 24: Time for our first tournament. All three debaters are eager to participate. After a twelve hour drive to Winfield, we are reminded by Coach Ed Trimmer that Lincoln–Douglas debate is second semester. Abbott Tublard consoles us on the return drive by describing Academy Award winning movies that he has memorized, line perfect.

Oct 15: Finally, we are accepted to a tournament! Our affirmative, proposing a new system called Medicare that we found in the Collier's Encyclopedia, appears unbeatable. The quotes from President Johnson are very convincing.

Oct 16: Alas, the affirmative failed! Our killer quote from President Eisenhower "The status quo is good" did not convince the judges. To uplift our spirits, Abbott Tublard promised to bring us his copy of *Bartlett's Quotations*. Thanks, Coach!

Nov 3: Wounds licked, we travel to Salina. Since overnight housing in motels is impossible on our debate budget of $10.56, Salina mentor Gary Harmon finds us private housing. The pigs and horses were friendly, but the kid being born in the middle of the night was murder! Once again, we make our opponents happy. One team even forgets to ask for their affirmative back after we ask for it in cross-ex! Abbott Tublard promises that the acolytes will copy it when we get back to the Wallow. Ecstasy rules!

Nov 20: Our affirmative on ozone depletion is ready! Wait til the honored opposition teams at the Topeka High tournament hear this!

Nov 22: Um, wrong topic. However, brothers Aetna and Cigna almost win a round. After watching the Manhattan teams in the champ final rounds at Salina, they checked out all the encyclopedias from the library, and carried them around in a freshly scrubbed livestock tank. Unfortunately, the unwieldy burden proved too much for them at the top of the third floor stairwell. After extracting themselves from the debris in the basement, they were five minutes late to their round, and therefore found themselves as the only team ever to lose to BYE. Goddesslike Coach Pam McComas consoles the boys with a free trip back down the stairs in record time! Boy, the big city! Nothing like it!

Dec 17: N.F.L. eve! We catch the bus to Great Bend and register! Wow, only forty-seven teams this year! The Clinton squared team makes plans for Kansas City in June!

Dec 19: Almost! Not Quite! But we did end up forty-fourth alternate to the three teams that did qualify! Sister Clinton says that she will keep clipping out the articles on health care from the Tribune during second semester, just in case!

Jan 5: Abbott Tublard turns in our new point sheets to N.F.L. national office. Let's see, we debated fifty four rounds, times 3.... heck, old Abbott Tublard only needs ninety four more seasons of highly successful debate like this to be a diamond coach!

Jan 12: Second semester begins! Moe, Larry and Curly celebrate by being suspended for smoking in the principal's office. Aren't they cute? Brother Castro supplied them with the cigars!

Feb 15: The D.I.'s are ready, just in time for the big Garden City tournament! Brother has *The Scarlet Ibis* down pat, after four years of running it. Sister Agnes is ready, but is unfortunately on maternity leave.

Feb 17: Sister Thatcher pulls a one ranking! We framed the ballot with the finest we could purchase at the Buffalo Wallow Art Supply and Liquor Store. We are still exultant, after the seventeen hour adventure back through the blizzard that caused all but Hutchinson and ourselves to cancel. Abbott Tublard says we have turned the corner! (as we slid off the Interstate).

Feb 24: Our first student congress of the year, at Pittsburg! All learn much, especially Sister Vixen, who disappears during a recess and never returns.

March 1: The top four qualifying debate teams for nats, all from Tornado High School, are disqualified for being over age forty! Only thirty nine alternates to go!

March 4: At the Colby tournament, Abbott Tublard chokes on an Oreo cookie in the coaches' lounge. He says that in the last seconds before passing out, the images of Moe, Larry and Curly appear before him. His resulting gag reflex clears his trachea, and now he's fine!

March 15: At Field Kindley High School in Coffeyville, Moe, Curly, and Larry all enter duo interp as the same team. No one notices. M, C, and L celebrate by tearing down the goalposts behind the school.

March 21: Sister Vixen reappears as the lead in a Hollywood movie, *Body of Evidence*.

March 22: Brother Castro causes a stir by advocating nuclear proliferation in a speech about bovine growth hormone.

March 24: Student Congress Eve! The ladies are all excited about the chance of giving an authorship speech to the Buffalo Wallow legislation "Ban Violence in Prayer in School."

March 25: In the coaches meeting, the Director of Forensics of the Wholesome Grains High School announces that the three teams that placed high in the December debate qualifier have all quit school to worship prairie grass fires. Only thirty-six left to go! Meanwhile, the girls give no speeches, but Prancer does get an offer of a date from a page named Rudolph! Her mother nixes the idea of a four hundred mile romance. Sorry, Prance!

March 30: Brother Biden wins oratory at the Blue Valley tournament! Exultation turns to despair as it is revealed that the brother had "borrowed" his speech from some dude named Churchill.

April 15: Wichita – Individual events N.F.L. eve! Our last chance to qualify somebody for Nationals in Kansas City. We think we're ready! The extempers have filed all the issues of *Useless News and World Distort* up through November, when Sister Gandhi's mom's subscription ran out. Sister Thatcher has her prep time down to only two hours for a two minute speech – go Maggie!

April 17: What a tourney. Brother Biden got two ones until someone who had read some Martin Luther King Jr. judged him! Sister Thatcher gave a great round two speech from her round one topic. And Moe, Larry and Curley pulled a four and a five when the three wild and crazy guys were

A Chronicle of the Plague Year

accidentally scheduled in the same section. The guys celebrate with a party at the Dew Drop Inn. The firefighters and police enjoy it immensely.

April 18: Well, no one qualified for nationals, but Acolyte Crisco did win a debate in Lincoln–Douglas! Crisco personally thanked the judges as they were helped back into their jackets and loaded back into the padded van.

May 1: Governor Finney closes the Shawnee Mission and BlueValley schools and sells them off to the highest bidder to finance a new governor's yacht to cruise Lake Perry. Thirty-three teams are eliminated from consideration by this action. Only one more team to go!

May 2: Moe, Larry and Curly find the address of the Lawrence team still left, with the aid of an English interpreter.

May 3: The Lawrence team resigns! We take up a collection for their hospitalization costs, and start fundraising for nationals!

June 15: We hit the road for Kansas City, with a planned stop off in Salina to visit a dog of which Brother Clinton has fond memories.

June 17: Round one at Nationals! Clinton squared walk in to a reunion! Brother Clinton's roommate from camp is their first round opponent! After first exchanging pleasantries, the ambulance removes their opponent. A bye! What a great tournament!

Respectfully submitted,
Scrivener Nathaniel

The Director of Humanity

(originally published 1995)

O.K., Coch, heir is the report yew tole me to rite.

Why I wuz assined to do: i wuz knot doin' tew well on the assinment to skedule the juges, but how wuz i to no that a juj shud not juj a person frum hiz own skool? Yew juj me awl the time, rite, Coch? Doan wurry. i still love yew. Yew R grate.

So, yew tole me to be in charge of GOOD DEEDS. i wuz very xsited to be in charge, un i wuz even mo xsited when yew tole me i wuz TOURNAMENT DIRECTOR 4 HUMANITY. Yew even rote it down 4 me! Thass why i wrote it down so purty — i copied it — thanks, Coch! But yew tole me to keep it a secret, un i did, un yew gave me twenty dollars un tole me to stay away from yew, beekose yew wood be busy — un i did, tew! But i new yew wood want to no how i spent yer $, so heir is a compleat akkounting!

7:30 AM i am sitting by the back door, just like Leesa tole me to, in case enny1 tries to come in that door. Un sure enuf, out comes a gurl, un o is she sick! She just heavin' un nuttin comin up, so i asks her to sit down un i talk to hur a whiles, un she talks back, un she sez she feels better, un i tried to buy hur a seben-up beekose my gram sez it does wunders fer a tetchy belly, but she sez no, so I save money! (yur money!) Then she tries to go back in, but Leesa, she done locked the door by mistake, prolly. So we walk round the skool, un their is loss of mudd, so we xchange shoos, well, relly she wears my shoos, un i walk in the mudd, but thass alright, i like it. Un when we git to the frunt, she takes hur shoos back un gives me a little hug —THANKS, COCH!

8:30 AM Leesa sez i am to go back to the back door in case enny jujs try to get in there. I tole her it wuz locked, un she sez she no it. So she tole me to go help the Biblical interpretation pipple over at the Church acros town. I am ashamed to admit I never got there, as yew will C, but i thot that the

TOURNAMENT DIRECTOR 4 HUMANITY wood be needed at the skool mo then the Church, un ennyways, 1 of the peeple i helped tole me that there wuzn't no Biblical interp ennyway, but Leesa, she wuz reelly upset un i am sure she just maid a mistake.

8:32 AM (i no bekaws i askd): a boy frum a skul neads hiz ty tyd. i do. He shakes my hand. THANKS, COCH!

8:34 AM: a gurl drops hur files fur a debait on the stairs. I pick up hur files fur hur, un brung em to hur between speeches. She gives me a piece of gum- THANKS, COCH!

9:30 AM: - two fellas R tryin to hawl their debait stuff up the stairs. i help. They doan even thank me, but thass okidoki - i no they wuz thankful.

9:32: i spend 50 sense to by a seben- up 4 a juj who feel bad after a debait. He tell me awl about it, un tho it doan make much sense to me, i nod my hed, un he finawly tell me i am a genus! THANKS, COCH!

10AM: i reckon, a boy is walkin in the hawl, talkin' to hisself. I ask him whut wuz the matter, un he still keep talkin'! So I just stand un lissen, un nod my head like i did with the juj, an he finaly pound me on the back un walks into a room, reel cocky like. He didn' thank me either, but it wuz ok, tew.

10 somethin' AM: A gurl sez she is hungry, so I by hur a baby ruthie. She sez i saved hur life! THANKS COCH!

11 somethin' or so AM: loss of pipple say dey R hungry, so i stand by the candy stuff un by them stuff. i spend almoss awl the money, but every 1 is reel happy, un they shake my hand, un 1 gurl even holes it 4 a bit -THANKS, COCH!

11 somethin or so: Bary from the consessun stand comes an yells at me fur hurtin his bizness. i by him a baby ruthie, un he sez i am incorjable. That is the 1st good thing Bary ever say! Maybe we can be frends?

12 - lunch!: I doan have enny money, but the juj i talked tew gives me a hole pizza he got someplace. Rite after thet, Marry Lew come past talkin' bout how awl the food iz gone from the jujs lozenge. i give her moss of the pizza, un she 8 it, since yew no Marry Lew- she is a BIG gurl un needs her daily bread. She... well... she gives me a little peck on the cheek, un that's awl it wuz, so F yew heir ennything else it is just a ly! She is a sweetie, tho! THANKS, COCH!

1 PM: Loss of foks waitin to see the postings, un they R gettin' a bit loud, so i tell some jokes my pa tells, un they awl laff. The none fron the cathllic skul doan look tew happy, but i tell the 1 about Martin Luther N the theological axident, Time do fli!

1:45 PM: Postin's, un dere awl sorts of pipple cussin' un screemin' un laffing, un a few cryin', so i sit un lissen to the ones who cryin' un nod my hed un say "yew rite", un soon they awl picks up un leafs. Some say thanks, un others doan, but i no they awl thankful.

3:30 PM: mo pipple in the hawl cryin, this time about stuff cawled kritiks. i lissen, un give 'em some advice from my pa - F yew doan like it, take it tew the corner stor! They git awl xcited, pound me on the back un rush off! Maybee i can do this debait stuff, huh, Coch? Jess think - i at nashunals! Yew n me, Coch!

5 PM: Leesa send me backstage during the awards, bekuse she needs me to present the booby prize. Then she 4git, un never awards it! But that wuz gud! i have a hole bunch of cryin' pipple, sayin' jujs had done NASTY things to them, so I am busy lissening.

10:30 PM: i Finnish helpin Nickalodeon the Custodian clean up the rooms, un then he gives me a ride home. He shakes my hand, n says i could grow up tew be juss like him! THANKS, COCH!

So, agin, thanks COCH! It wuz jess about the finest day of my life! Un loss of pipple thot i wuz jus hangin' around doin' nuttin!

(spelling korrekted by hiz muther)

The Director of Humanity